AMS SHORT COURSE LECTURE NOTES
Introductory Survey Lectures
A Subseries of Proceedings of Symposia in Applied Mathematics

PROCEEDINGS OF SYMPOSIA IN APPLIED MATHEMATICS

AMS SHORT COURSE LECTURE NOTES

Introductory Survey Lectures

published as a subseries of
Proceedings of Symposia in Applied Mathematics

PROCEEDINGS OF SYMPOSIA
IN APPLIED MATHEMATICS
Volume 39

Chaos and Fractals
The Mathematics Behind
the Computer Graphics

Robert L. Devaney and Linda Keen, Editors

Kathleen T. Alligood and James A. Yorke
Michael F. Barnsley
Bodil Branner
Jenny Harrison
Philip J. Holmes

American Mathematical Society
Providence, Rhode Island

LECTURE NOTES PREPARED FOR THE
AMERICAN MATHEMATICAL SOCIETY SHORT COURSE
CHAOS AND FRACTALS
THE MATHEMATICS BEHIND THE COMPUTER GRAPHICS
HELD IN PROVIDENCE, RHODE ISLAND
AUGUST 6–7, 1988

The AMS Short Course Series is sponsored by the Society's Committee on Employment and Educational Policy (CEEP). The series is under the direction of the Short Course Advisory Subcommittee of CEEP.

Library of Congress Cataloging-in-Publication Data

Chaos and fractals: the mathematics behind the computer graphics/Robert L. Devaney and Linda Keen, editors: [authors] Kathleen T. Alligood...[et al.]

    p. cm. – (Proceedings of symposia in applied mathematics, ISSN 0160-7634; v. 39. American Mathematical Society short course series)

    "Synopses of the talks and lecture notes...published in the April 1988 issue of the Notices of the American Mathematical Society on pages 597–599 and are reprinted here."

    Includes bibliographical references and indexes.

    Contents: Overview: dynamics of simple maps/Robert L. Devaney–Nonlinear oscillations and the Smale horseshoe map/Philip J. Holmes–Fractal basin boundaries and chaotic attractors/Kathleen T. Alligood and James A. Yorke–Julia Sets/Linda Keen–The Mandelbrot set/Bodil Branner–Introduction to fractals/Jenny Harrison–Iterated function systems/Michael F. Barnsley.

    ISBN 0-8218-0137-6 (alk. paper)

    1. Computer graphics–Mathematics. 2. Fractals. I. Devaney, Robert L., 1948- . II. Keen, Linda. III. Alligood, Kathleen. IV. Series: Proceedings of symposia in applied mathematics; v. 39. V. Series: Proceedings of symposia in applied mathematics. AMS short course lecture notes.

T385.C454 1989   89-7003
006.6–dc20   CIP

1980 *Mathematics Subject Classification.* (1985 *Revision*).
Primary 58F99; Secondary 30C99, 34C35, 51M99.
Copyright © 1989 by the American Mathematical Society. All rights reserved.
Printed in the United States of America.
The paper used in this book is acid-free and falls within the guidelines
established to ensure permanence and durability. ∞

This publication was typeset using $\mathcal{A}_{\mathcal{M}}\mathcal{S}$-T$_{\!E}$X,
the American Mathematical Society's T$_{\!E}$X macro system.

10 9 8 7 6 5 4 3 2 1   94 93 92 91 90 89

Table of Contents

Preface

The concepts of *chaos* and *fractal* have become quite popular in recent years, even among people with little mathematical background. Among the reasons for this surge of interest are the publication of several books and articles intended for general audiences. These include James Gleick's *Chaos: Making a New Science* and articles in Scientific American showing the great beauty of the computer graphics images of complex dynamical systems. At times, all the attention devoted to these topics seems to obscure the fact that there really is some beautiful mathematics in the fields of chaotic dynamical systems and fractal geometry. The goal of the Short Course at which these lectures were given was to remedy this.

The course was called *Chaos and Fractals*: *The Mathematics Behind the Computer Graphics* and was organized at the Centennial Meeting of the American Mathematical Society held in Providence, RI, on August 6–7, 1988. The lectures covered a wide range of topics from dynamical systems and fractal geometry. Among many other concepts, the lectures covered the period doubling route to chaos, Smale's horseshoe and symbolic dynamics, strange attractors and their basin boundaries, Julia sets and the Mandelbrot set, Hausdorff and entropy dimension, and applications in engineering and data compression. This book contains expanded versions of the seven lectures delivered during the Short Course.

We would especially like to thank Jim Maxwell, Monica Foulkes, and their staffs from the American Mathematical Society, who coordinated the Short Course. With over 550 participants, this course was the largest in AMS history. Despite the memorable 100° temperatures during the course, we were very pleased with the results.

Robert L. Devaney
Linda Keen

Proceedings of Symposia in Applied Mathematics
Volume **39**, 1989

Dynamics of Simple Maps

ROBERT L. DEVANEY

Our goal in this paper is to introduce, in as simple a setting as possible, some of the fundamental ideas of dynamics. These ideas include the notions of chaos and fractal, two often used and abused words in contemporary mathematical jargon. Our aim is to show how these terms arise naturally in the field of dynamical systems.

One of the great breakthroughs in dynamics in the past few decades has been the realization that even the simplest of dynamical systems may behave extremely unpredictably. The quadratic map of the real line given by $x \to x^2 + c$ where c is a real parameter is typical. Certainly there is no simpler nonlinear dynamical process than iteration of this function. Yet, as we will see, there are many c-values where the dynamics of this map are extremely complicated.

When we pass to the complex plane, the mapping $z \to z^2 + c$ is the setting for the beautiful recent mathematical work of Mandelbrot and Douady and Hubbard. For these maps, the plane decomposes into two distinct subsets, the stable set, on which the dynamics are tame and well understood, and the Julia set, on which the dynamics are quite chaotic and complicated (yet, thanks to recent work, fairly well understood). The contributions of Keen and Branner in this volume delve in more detail into these issues.

The place where one finds complicated dynamics is often a fractal. This is almost always true in the case of Julia sets, and in many other settings as well, including the basin boundaries studied by Yorke and Alligood and the "horseshoe" mappings described by Holmes in this volume. More details on fractals and some of their applications are described by Harrison and Barnsley in this volume as well.

Our goal in this paper is to lay the foundation for these later contributions. We will introduce a number of fundamental dynamical notions in the setting of one-dimensional dynamics. These notions include the notions of periodic

1980 *Mathematics Subject Classification* (1985 *Revision*). Primary 58F13; Secondary 58F14, 30C99.

and chaotic behavior, symbolic dynamics, and basic bifurcation theory. The complicated dynamics that occur in one-dimensional dynamics will be shown to occur most frequently on the most basic fractal of all, a Cantor set. We will use symbolic dynamics to show how these dynamics may be analyzed completely.

Finally, in the last section, we describe Sarkovskii's Theorem, a striking and powerful theorem which has become one of the centerpieces of one dimensional dynamics.

I would like to thank Mark Meyerson and Sue Staples for pointing out a number of errors in the original version of this paper.

1. Iteration. Let $F : \mathbf{R} \to \mathbf{R}$ be a smooth function. Our goal will be to describe the dynamics of F. This means that we are interested in the behavior of points under iteration of F. We will denote the nth iterate of F by F^n. That is,

$$F^2 = F \circ F,$$
$$F^3 = F \circ F \circ F,$$

and so forth.

If $p \in \mathbf{R}$, the sequence of points

$$p, \ F(p), \ F^2(p), \ldots$$

is called the orbit of p. The main question in dynamics is can one predict the fate of all orbits of F? That is, what can be said about the behavior of $F^n(p)$ as $n \to \infty$? As we shall see, even for simple quadratic maps of the real line the answer to this question is quite difficult, but extremely interesting.

Before discussing the behavior of orbits, let us make a slight digression to explain where this type of dynamics comes from. Basically, the study of iterated maps has evolved from a desire to understand the behavior of solutions of ordinary differential equations. Differential equations give rise to iterated maps in two different ways. One way is via numerical solution. Virtually any scheme for integrating a differential equation numerically (such as Runge-Kutta) reduces to an iterative procedure or a mapping. Another technique for reducing a differential equation to a map occurs when there is a surface of section or cross-section present for the flow. This occurs when all solution curves repeatedly intersect a submanifold of codimension one as depicted in Figure 1.1. To understand the behavior of solution curves, it suffices to understand the iterates of the *first return map* which associates to a given point p in the surface the next point of intersection $F(p)$ of the solution curve through p with the surface. The map in this case is called a *Poincaré map*. While the study of maps in place of differential equations predates Poincaré, he was the mathematician who first really exploited the study of maps.

Iteration also arises in many areas naturally, without coming from a differential equation. For example, consider the following simple example from

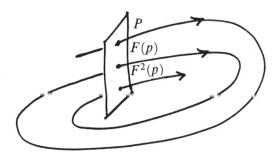

FIGURE 1.1. A surface of section.

ecology. Suppose the population of a single species reproducing in a con-trolled environment has population at generation n given by P_n. To keep the numbers manageable, let us assume that P_n represents the percentage of some a priori upper bound for the population, so $0 \le P_n \le 1$. For the ecologist, the important problem is to construct a mathematical model which allows him or her to predict the ultimate behavior of the population. Will the population die out or will it tend to stabilize at some limiting value? Or will it change cyclically or behave in some other, more random fashion?

One of the simplest models of population growth used in ecology is the *logistic equation*. This equation is given by

$$P_{n+1} = k \, P_n(1 - P_n).$$

Here k is a constant which depends on ecological conditions. Given this equation, it would seem to be a straightforward problem to predict the ul-timate behavior of P_n given some initial population P_0. As we shall see, however, this is far from the case for certain k-values.

Note that, if we let $F(x) = kx(1 - x)$, then the solution of the logistic equation for a given initial population P_0 is equivalent to computing the orbit of P_0:

$$P_0, \ P_1 = F(P_0), \ P_2 = F^2(P_0), \dots .$$

Much of our work in this paper will deal with this function or other quadratic analogues.

Now let us return to the study of the dynamics of $F : \mathbf{R} \to \mathbf{R}$. Computing orbits is most easily done with a computer, or, in our simple setting, even with a calculator. For example, if $F(x) = x^2$, it is clear that

$$F^n(x) \to \infty \quad \text{if } |x| > 1,$$
$$F^n(x) \to 0 \quad \text{if} |x| < 1,$$
$$F^n(1) = 1 \quad \text{for all } n,$$
$$F^n(-1) = 1 \quad \text{if } n \ge 1.$$

That is, all orbits are asymptotic either to ∞ or to 0, except 1, which is a *fixed point*, or -1, which is *eventually fixed*. Actually, 0 is also a fixed point.

Note that there is a difference between the fixed points at 0 and 1. 0 is an *attracting fixed point* or *sink*, since nearby points have orbits which tend to 0. 1, on the other hand, is a *repelling fixed point* or *source*, since nearby orbits tend away from 1.

Another simple example is provided by the square root function $T(x) = \sqrt{x}$. Since

$$T^n(x) \to 1$$

for all $x > 0$, 1 is an attracting fixed point. $S(x) = \sin x$ in radians similarly has 0 as an attracting fixed point which attracts all orbits. Of course, $\pi, 2\pi, 3\pi, \ldots$ are all eventually fixed points. Note that orbits take a very long time to reach 0 under iteration of S; although 0 is an attracting fixed point, it is a "weak" attractor for reasons we will explore in a moment. A final example which is quite interesting for its unexpected result is cosine. What happens when $C(x) = \cos x$ is iterated? With a calculator one sees immediately that all orbits tend to .73908.... This comes as kind of a surprise to the uninitiated, but we will see below that this point is nothing but another attracting fixed point.

At this point it would seem that the dynamics of one-dimensional maps is not very interesting. But just wait, for nothing could be further from the truth!

A simple technique for studying one-dimensional dynamics is *graphical analysis*. This technique allows us to predict the qualitative behavior of orbits from a knowledge of the graph of a function. To compute the orbit of a point x under iteration of F, one simply draws the diagonal $y = x$ as well as the graph of F, and then repeats the following procedure over and over. If we draw a vertical line from (x, x) to the graph of F, followed by a horizontal line back to the diagonal, then we reach the point $(F(x), F(x))$. Repeating this process yields the point $(F^2(x), F^2(x))$. Continuing, we see that the orbit of x is displayed along the diagonal. Figure 1.2 displays graphical analysis as applied to $T(x) = \sqrt{x}$ and $C(x) = \cos x$.

As a parenthetical remark, we note that all of the above concepts—iteration, especially with a calculator or computer, and graphical analysis—can be taught to precalculus students. It is my belief that this area of mathematics presents a real opportunity to present contemporary mathematical ideas to an unsophisticated audience. When coupled with the alluring computer graphics which arise quite naturally in dynamics, the prospects for exciting students about mathematics are quite good! Enough moralizing...

Graphical analysis allows us to understand what makes certain fixed points attracting and others repelling. If the derivative of F at the fixed point is less than 1 in absolute value, then that fixed point is attracting. If the absolute value of the derivative is larger than 1, then the fixed point is repelling. See

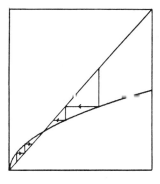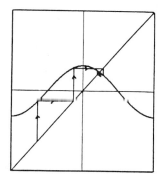

FIGURE 1.2. Graphical analysis of $T(x) = \sqrt{x}$ and $C(x) = \cos x$.

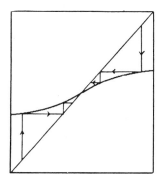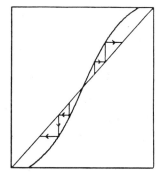

FIGURE 1.3. Attracting and repelling fixed points.

Figure 1.3. This is a nice application of dynamics that can easily be conveyed in a calculus course.

At this point, let us consider several more examples. Let

$$T_{-1}(x) = x^2 - 1.$$

It is useful at this point to write a short computer program to iterate a function like T_{-1}. The code, especially in BASIC, is quite easy to write (6 lines long) and immediately produces a list of the orbit of an initial input x_0. One sees immediately that certain orbits tend to ∞, while other orbits tend to oscillate between values near 0 and -1.

Graphical analysis (Figure 1.4) confirms this. T_{-1} has two fixed points, the roots of

$$x^2 - 1 = x.$$

Let x_+ denote the positive fixed point. Then x_+ is repelling and, indeed, if $|x| > x_+$, the orbit of x tends to ∞. On the other hand, we have

$$T_{-1}(0) = -1, \qquad T_{-1}(-1) = 0$$

so we say that 0 and -1 lie on a *periodic orbit* or *cycle of period* 2. Note that this orbit is an attracting orbit, because if x is close to 0 or -1, then the orbit of x tends to the periodic orbit.

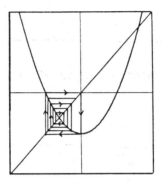

FIGURE 1.4. Graphical analysis of $T_{-1}(x) = x^2 - 1$.

At this point we urge the reader to write a computer program which computes orbits of various functions. You will see a vast array of different dynamical behavior if you compute the orbits of various x-values for $T_c(x) = x^2 + c$ where

1. $c = -1.1$,
2. $c = -1.3$ (period 4),
3. $c = -1.38$ (period 8),
4. $c = -1.395$ (period 16),
5. $c = -1.755$ (period 3),
6. $c = -2$,
7. $c = -3$.

As a remark, we note that it appears that, in case 5, all orbits tend either to a periodic orbit of period 3 or to ∞. Similarly, it appears in case 7 that all orbits tend to ∞. In both cases, however, this observed behavior is quite misleading. Much more is actually going on!

We close this section by formalizing several definitions.

DEFINITION. Let $F : \mathbf{R} \to \mathbf{R}$. The point x_0 is a fixed point for F if $F(x_0) = x_0$. The point x_0 is a periodic point of period n for F if $F^n(x_0) = x_0$ but $F^i(x_0) \neq x_0$ for $0 < i < n$. The point x_0 is eventually periodic if $F^n(x_0) = F^{n+m}(x_0)$, but x_0 is not itself periodic.

DEFINITION. A periodic point x_0 of period n is attracting if $|(F^n)'(x_0)| < 1$. The periodic point x_0 is repelling if $|(F^n)'(x_0)| > 1$. x_0 is neutral if $|(F^n)'(x_0)| = 1$.

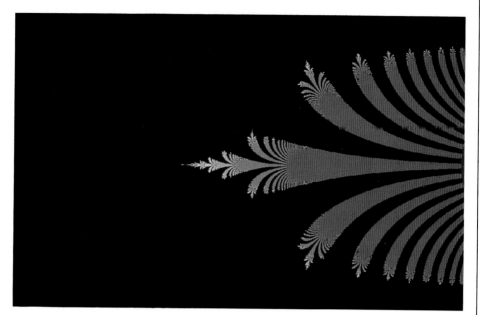

COLOR PLATE 1

COLOR PLATE 2

Color Plates 1 and 2 show the explosion in the exponential family λe^z (Julia sets for $.36e^z$ and $.38e^z$).

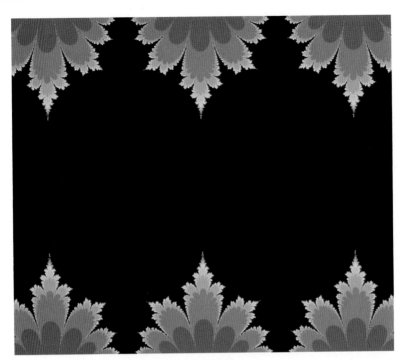

COLOR PLATE 3

COLOR PLATE 4

Color Plates 3 *and* 4 *show the explosion in the cosine family* $\lambda \cos z$ *(Julia sets for* $.66i \cos z$ *and* $.68i \cos z$*).*

2. The quadratic family. In this section we will begin the study of the family of quadratic maps given by

$$F_c(x) = x^2 + c.$$

We will describe in detail what happens when c decreases. In a very real sense, this family contains virtually all of the complications of higher dimensional dynamics (except strange attractors) in the simplest possible setting.

Our first observation is that if $c > 1/4$, then the graph of F_c lies above the diagonal. Graphical analysis therefore shows that

$$F_c^n(x) \to \infty$$

for all $x \in \mathbf{R}$.

When $c = 1/4$, the graph of F_c is tangent to the diagonal at $x = 1/2$. For $c < 1/4$, F_c has two fixed points given by the roots of

$$x^2 + c = x.$$

We will denote the larger fixed point by p_+ and the smaller by p_-.

For $-3/4 < c < 1/4$, one may check easily that

$$|F_c'(p_-)| < 1$$

while

$$|F_c'(p_-)| > 1$$

if $c < -3/4$. Also,

$$F_c'(p_+) > 1$$

for all $c < 1/4$. Note that, by graphical analysis, if $x \in (-p_+, p_+)$, and $-3/4 < c < 1/4$, then

$$F_c^n(x) \to p_-.$$

If $|x| > p_+$, then

$$F_c^n(x) \to \infty.$$

This is our first example of a *bifurcation*. As c decreases through $1/4$, a new fixed point for F_c appears (a neutral fixed point) which then immediately splits into two fixed points, $p_\pm$, one attracting and one repelling. This simple bifurcation is called a *saddle node bifurcation*. See Figure 2.1.

Graphical analysis also shows that, for all $c < 1/4$, if $|x| > p_+$ then $F_c^n(x) \to \infty$. We will therefore restrict our attention to the interval I_c given by $[-p_+, p_+]$; all of the interesting dynamics of F_c occur in I_c.

The next bifurcation for this family occurs when $c = -3/4$. The reader may check that, when $c = -3/4$,

$$F_c'(p_-) = -1,$$

so p_- is a neutral fixed point. For this map, it is still true that all orbits of points in $(-p_+, p_+)$ tend to p_-. However, when c passes through $-3/4$, two things occur. First, the fixed point at p_- becomes repelling. Second, a new

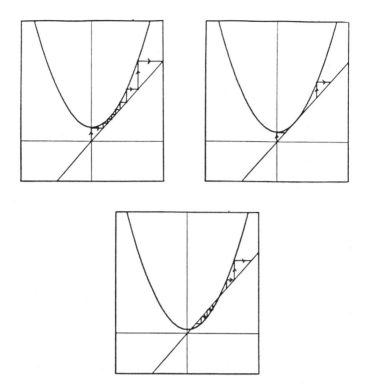

FIGURE 2.1. The saddle-node bifurcation at $c = 1/4$.

periodic orbit of period two appears, and, for $-5/4 < c < -3/4$, this periodic orbit is itself attracting.

The easiest way to see this is to sketch the graph of $F_c^2(x)$ where

$$F_c^2(x) = (x^2 + c)^2 + c.$$

The graphs of F_c^2 are depicted in Figure 2.2.

This bifurcation is called the period-doubling bifurcation. In this bifurcation, a fixed or periodic point changes from attracting to repelling (through derivative -1) while a new attracting periodic orbit of twice its period is born.

One can, in this case, compute the roots of $F_c^2(x) = x$ exactly, since this is a polynomial equation of degree four, two of whose roots are already known. However, finding other periodic points of higher period in this manner is a hopeless task. For this reason, we will resort to qualitative methods such as graphical analysis for the remainder of this section.

The key to understanding what happens next as c decreases is to look at the graphs of F_c and F_c^2. In Figure 2.3 we have plotted these graphs for various c-values. Note that we have enclosed a portion of the graph of F_c^2 in a small box. In this box, the graph of F_c^2 "resembles" the graph of F_c. Indeed, as c

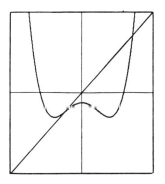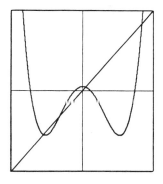

FIGURE 2.2. The graph of $F_c^2(x)$ for $c > -3/4$ and $c < -3/4$.

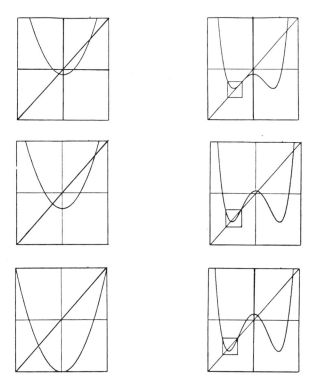

FIGURE 2.3. Graphs of F_c, F_c^2 for c-values near $-3/4$.

decreases, the portion of the graph of F_c^2 in the box develops a hump exactly as F_c has done. We therefore expect that F_c^2 will behave dynamically in this small region exactly as F_c has in the larger interval. That is, we expect that the attracting fixed point for F_c^2 (actually a period two point) will eventually attain derivative -1. Then we expect that F_c^2 will itself undergo a period doubling bifurcation, producing, as the period 2 orbit becomes repelling, a new attracting orbit of period 4.

We will not prove that this in fact does happen here. Rather, we will defer to an amazing result of Sarkovskii which we will discuss later. While this theorem will not exactly lead to a proof of this result, it will provide a lot of evidence for its truth.

Note that the process of looking at the graph of F_c^2 in a little box can now be repeated for F_c^4. This means that we expect the period 4 orbit to period-double eventually, producing a new attracting periodic orbit of period 8. Continuing, we expect a sequence of c-values, $c_1, c_2, c_3, \ldots$, at which F_c undergoes a period doubling bifurcation and a new periodic orbit of period 2^n arises. This is, in fact, what happens.

At this point we urge the reader to experiment with the computer by iterating F_c on I_c. One sees quite clearly the first few period doublings. However, eventually, the period 2^n orbits seem to disappear and orbits begin to behave erratically, without ever converging to a periodic orbit.

This sequence of bifurcations has been called the *period-doubling route to chaos*. It has been observed in many different dynamical settings. Indeed, any smooth one-dimensional map must undergo a similar sequence of bifurcations as the dynamics become more complex.

EXAMPLE. We urge the reader to experiment with the families $x \mapsto cx(1 - x)$ with $0 < c \leq 4$ and $x \mapsto c \sin x$ with $0 < c \leq \pi$. Similar phenomena occur for both families.

As another remark, the process of examining F_c^2 in a small box and noting its similarity with the graphs of F_c in the large is precisely the renormalization group analysis popularized by Feigenbaum [F] in the mid-seventies. He used this process to suggest that the succession of period doubling bifurcations we just observed occurs at a universal rate which is essentially independent of the particular family of maps.

The natural question at this point is what happens at the limit of this period doubling sequence. Rather than discuss this difficult question, let us jump ahead a bit to the parameter value $c = -2$. We ask the question how many periodic points does F_{-2} have? Note that the fixed points for F_{-2} are 2 and -1. Hence the interval I_{-2} is $[-2, 2]$. The graph of F_{-2} on this interval is displayed in Figure 2.4. Note that $F_{-2}(0) = -2$, so that $F_{-2}^2(0) = 2$, i.e., 0 is eventually fixed. Note also that F_{-2} maps each subinterval $[-2, 0]$ and $[0, 2]$ over the entire interval $[-2, 2]$. That is, F_{-2} folds I_c over itself twice.

As a consequence, it follows that F_{-2}^2 folds I_{-2} over itself 4 times, F_{-2}^3 folds I_2 8 times, and, in general, F_{-2}^n folds I_{-2} over itself 2^n times. The graphs of various F_{-2}^n are shown in Figure 2.4. We see from the graphs that F_{-2}^n has exactly 2^n fixed points for each n. This means that as c decreases, the number of periodic orbits increases dramatically. Note that we have found a

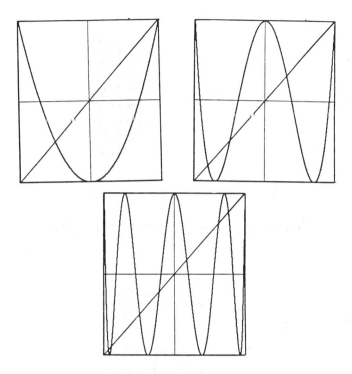

FIGURE 2.4. The graphs of F_{-2}, F_{-2}^2 and F_{-2}^3.

lot more periodic orbits for $c = -2$ than the period-doubled orbits we found earlier. For example, there are 32 fixed points of F_{-2}^5. These are the two original fixed points $p_\pm$ and 6 periodic orbits of period 5, none of which have period-doubled since their period is odd.

So, the question becomes, where have all these periodic points come from? We will return to this question over and over again in the sequel.

At this point, we again suggest that the reader experiment with a computer. It is instructive to plot the orbit of 0 for various c-values. This is what we have done in Figure 2.5. We have plotted the last 100 of 150 iterates of 0 for 300 equally spaced c-values between $1/4$ and -2. We see quite clearly that the orbit of 0 converges to a fixed point for $-3/4 < c < 1/4$. Then we see the succession of period doubling bifurcations. This is followed by a succession of bounds in which the orbit of 0 appears random. These are the chaotic bands. Among these bands are interspersed "windows" where the orbit of 0 is again attracted to a periodic orbit. What is interesting about this diagram is that the same picture is obtained with virtually any inital x value (as long as $x \in I_c$). This is called the *bifurcation diagram* of F_c.

In Figure 2.6, we show a magnification of the period doubling regime for F_c, while in Figure 2.7 we expand the period 3 window.

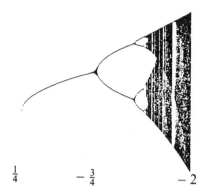

$$\frac{1}{4} \qquad\qquad -\frac{3}{4} \qquad\qquad -2$$

FIGURE 2.5. The bifurcation diagram of F_c.

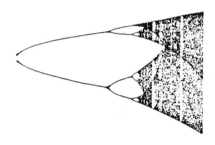

FIGURE 2.6. The period-doubling regime for F_c.

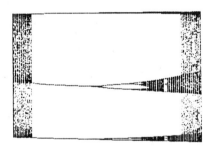

FIGURE 2.7. The period 3 window.

We finally remark that the bifurcation diagram is intimately related to the Mandelbrot set as discussed by Branner in this volume.

3. Symbolic dynamics. In this section we discuss the dynamics of F_c for c-values satisfying $c < -2$. We suggest that the reader begin by iterating one of these maps on the computer. Most likely, no matter which initial value is chosen, it appears that the orbit tends to ∞. As we will see, this is by no means true.

Throughout this section we will fix a particular c-value, $c < -2$. So we will drop the subscript on both F_c and I_c. The graph of F is shown in Figure 3.1. Note that the graph of F pokes through the bottom of the square centered at 0 with vertices at (p_+, p_+) and $(-p_+, -p_+)$. This means that certain orbits escape from I under iteration. Let A_0 denote the open interval which consists of points x for which $F(x) < -p_+$. As we saw above, when $x \in A_0$, since $F(x) \notin I$, the orbit of x tends to ∞. Hence, all of the interesting dynamics of F occurs in $I - A_0$. Moreover, F maps each of the two subintervals in $I - A_0$ onto the entire interval I.

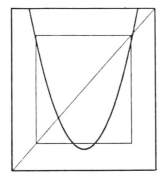

FIGURE 3.1. The graph of F.

Since F maps each subinterval in $I - A_0$ monotonically over I, it follows that there is an open interval in each which consists of points mapped into A_0 by F. Call the union of these two subintervals A_1. If $x \in A_1$ then $F(x) \in A_0$, so $F^2(x) < -p_+$ and it follows that $F^n(x) \to \infty$. Hence all of the interesting dynamics occur on $I - (A_0 \cup A_1)$. Continuing in the same manner, we note that F^2 maps each of the four intervals in $I - (A_0 \cup A_1)$ onto all of I, so there are four subintervals which contain points whose orbits leave I after 3 iterations. Hence we remove these four open intervals as well.

Continuing, we see that there are precisely 2^n open intervals which consist of points whose orbits escape from I after $n + 1$ iterations. The reader will recognize that the process of throwing away these successive collections of open intervals is precisely the same as the construction of the Cantor middle-thirds set (only we don't remove middle-thirds, just middle portions). This is indeed the case.

We will prove this only in case c is sufficiently negative. There exists c_* such that, for $c < c_*$,

$$|F_c'(x)| > 1$$

for $x \in I - A_0$. Let

$$\Lambda = \{x \in I | F^n(x) \in I \text{ for all } n \geq 0\}.$$

Λ consists of all points which never escape from I under iteration.

THEOREM. *If $c \leq c_*$, then Λ is a Cantor set.*

PROOF. Λ is closed since it is the nested intersection of closed sets. To see that Λ is totally disconnected, assume that the interval $[x, y] \subset \Lambda$. Then $A_0 \cap F^n[x, y] = \varnothing$ for all n, for otherwise certain points in $[x, y]$ would escape. Now $|F'(z)| > \lambda > 1$ for all $z \in I - A_0$. Therefore, $|(F^n)'(z)| > \lambda^n$ for all $z \in [x, y]$ by the chain rule. Therefore, by the Mean Value Theorem, F^n expands the interval $[x, y]$ by a factor of λ^n, and consequently, $x = y$. (Otherwise, some image of $[x, y]$ would overlap A_0.) Finally, to show that Λ is perfect, we observe that if $x \in \Lambda$, then x is a limit point of the various A_n's. To see this, choose any open interval containing x. The above argument shows that F^n expands this interval until some point (besides x) is mapped onto an endpoint of A_0. These endpoints are eventually fixed, and thus in Λ, so x is a limit point of such points.

q.e.d.

We remark that this fact is true for all $c < -2$, but we will not prove this here. Λ is an example of a "fractal" (see the papers of Barnsley and Harrison in this volume). Thus we see that fractals occur quite naturally in the dynamics of the simplest functions. Indeed, they occur quite often as the setting in which all of the "interesting" dynamics takes place.

We therefore see that the dynamics of F are quite simple on $\mathbf{R} - \Lambda$: all orbits simply tend to ∞ on this set. But what about the dynamics on Λ? This is where symbolic dynamics enters the picture.

To understand the dynamics of F on Λ we will introduce a model mapping which captures all the essential ingredients of $F|\Lambda$. To construct this model, we first define

$$\Sigma = \{(s_0 s_1 s_2 \cdots) | s_j = 0 \text{ or } 1\}.$$

Σ is the space which consists of all infinite sequences of 0's and 1's.

We make Σ into a metric space as follows. Let $s = (s_0 s_1 s_2 \cdots)$ and $t = (t_0 t_1 t_2 \cdots)$. We define the distance

$$d[s, t] = \sum_{i=0}^{\infty} \frac{|s_i - t_i|}{2^i}.$$

The reader may easily check that d is a metric on Σ.

We now define the model mapping on Σ. Let $\sigma : \Sigma \to \Sigma$ be given by

$$\sigma(s_0 s_1 s_2 \cdots) = (s_1 s_2 s_3 \cdots).$$

That is, σ simply "forgets" the first entry of the sequence. The map σ is called the *shift automorphism*. We will see that σ "captures" all of the dynamical behavior of F on Λ. To prove that σ is continuous, we need a preliminary result.

LEMMA. *Let* $s, t \in \Sigma$, *with* $s = (s_0 s_1 s_2 \cdots)$ *and* $t = (t_0 t_1 t_2 \cdots)$. *Suppose* $s_i = t_i$ *for* $i = 0, 1, \ldots, n$. *Then* $d[s, t] \leq 1/2^n$. *Conversely, if* $d[s, t] < 1/2^n$, *then* $s_i = t_i$ *for* $i \leq n$.

PROOF. If $s_i = t_i$ for $i \leq n$, then

$$d[s, t] = \sum_{i=0}^{n} \frac{|s_i - s_i|}{2^i} + \sum_{i=n+1}^{\infty} \frac{|s_i - t_i|}{2^i} \leq \frac{1}{2^n}.$$

On the other hand, if $s_j \neq t_j$ for some $j \leq n$, then we must have

$$d[s, t] \geq \frac{1}{2^j} \geq \frac{1}{2^n}.$$

Consequently, if $d[s, t] < 1/2^n$, then $s_i = t_i$ for $i \leq n$.

q.e.d.

Now we may prove

PROPOSITION. *The shift automorphism* $\sigma : \Sigma \to \Sigma$ *is continuous.*

PROOF. Let $\epsilon > 0$ and $s = (s_0 s_1 s_2 \cdots)$. Pick n with $1/2^n < \epsilon$. Let $\delta = 1/2^{n+1}$. If $t = (t_0 t_1 t_2 \cdots)$ satisfies $d[s, t] < \delta$, then by the lemma we have $s_i = t_i$ for $i \leq n + 1$. Therefore

$$d[\sigma(s), \sigma(t)] \leq 1/2^n < \epsilon.$$

q.e.d.

What is the relationship between σ and F? To describe this, we recall that the interval I is divided into two closed subintervals when we remove A_0. Let us call these intervals I_0 and I_1. Recall that if $x \in \Lambda$, then $F^n(x) \in I_0 \cup I_1$ for all $n \geq 0$. Hence we may define the *itinerary* x by

$$S(x) = (s_0 s_1 s_2 \cdots)$$

where $s_j = 0$ or 1 and $s_j = k$ iff $F^j(x) \in I_k$.

THEOREM. *If* $c < c_+$, *then* $S : \Lambda \to \Sigma$ *is a homeomorphism.*

PROOF. We first show that S is one-to-one. Let $x, y \in \Lambda$ and suppose $S(x) = S(y)$. Then, for each n, $F^n(x)$ and $F^n(y)$ lie on the same side of A_0. It follows that F is monotonic on the interval between $F^n(x)$ and $F^n(y)$. Consequently, all points in this interval remain in $I_0 \cup I_1$. This contradicts the fact that Λ is totally disconnected.

To see that S is onto, we set, for a closed interval J,

$$F^{-n}(J) = \{x \in I \mid F^n(x) \in J\}.$$

Observe that if $J \subset I$ is a closed interval, then $F^{-1}(J)$ consists of two subintervals, one in I_0 and one in I_1. Let $s \in \Sigma$, with $s = (s_0 s_1 s_2 \cdots)$. We define

$$I_{s_0 s_1 \ldots s_n} = \{x \in I \mid x \in I_{s_0}, F(x) \in I_{s_1}, \ldots, F^n(x) \in I_{s_n}\}$$
$$= I_{s_0} \cap F^{-1}(I_{s_1}) \cap \cdots \cap F^{-n}(I_{s_n}).$$

We claim that the $I_{s_0...s_n}$ form a nested sequence of nonempty closed intervals as $n \to \infty$. Note that

$$I_{s_0...s_n} = I_{s_0} \cap F^{-1}(I_{s_1...s_n}).$$

By induction, we may assume that $I_{s_1...s_n}$ is a nonempty closed subinterval, so that $F^{-1}(I_{s_1...s_n})$ consists of two subintervals, one in I_0 and one in I_1. Hence $I_{s_0...s_n}$ is a single closed interval.

These intervals are nested because

$$I_{s_0...s_n} = I_{s_0...s_{n-1}} \cap F^{-n}(I_{s_n}) \subset I_{s_0...s_{n-1}}.$$

Thus we conclude that

$$\bigcap_{n \geq 0} I_{s_0...s_n}$$

is nonempty. Note that if $x \in \bigcap_{n \geq 0} I_{s_0 \cdots s_n}$, then $x \in I_{s_0}$, $F(x) \in I_{s_1}$, etc., so $S(x) = (s_0 s_1 s_2 \ldots)$. This proves that S is onto.

Note that $\bigcap_{n \geq 0} I_{s_0...s_n}$ consists of a unique point. This follows since S is one-to-one. In particular, diam $I_{s_0...s_n} \to 0$ as $n \to \infty$.

Finally, to prove continuity of S, we choose $x \in \Lambda$ and suppose that $S(x) = (s_0 s_1 s_2 \cdots)$. Let $\epsilon > 0$. Pick n so that $1/2^n < \epsilon$. Consider the $I_{t_0...t_n}$ for all possible combinations of $t_0, t_1, \ldots, t_n$. These subintervals are disjoint and Λ is contained in their union. There are 2^{n+1} such subintervals and $I_{s_0...s_n}$ is one of them. Hence we may choose δ such that $|x - y| < \delta$ and $y \in \Lambda$ implies that $y \in I_{s_0...s_n}$. Therefore $S(x)$ and $S(y)$ agree for the first $n + 1$ terms. By the lemma

$$d[S(x), S(y)] < 1/2^n < \epsilon.$$

This proves that S is continuous. It is easy to prove that S^{-1} is also continuous. Thus, S is a homeomorphism.

$$\text{q.e.d.}$$

Again, the above result is true for all $c < c_*$, but the proof is more complicated. Note that S gives the following commutative diagram:

$$
\begin{array}{ccc}
\Lambda & \xrightarrow{F} & \Lambda \\
S \downarrow & & \downarrow S \\
\Sigma & \xrightarrow{\sigma} & \Sigma
\end{array}
$$

We say that S gives a conjugacy between F and σ. S preserves virtually all dynamical properties since S preserves orbits, i.e., $\sigma^n \circ S(x) = S \circ F^n(x)$. In particular, periodic orbits of F and repeating sequences in Σ are in one-to-one correspondence. Hence there are precisely 2^n fixed points for F^n.

The map S carries dense subsets of Λ to dense subsets of Σ, and vice versa. We claim that the set of periodic sequences in Σ is dense. This follows since we may approximate an arbitrary sequence $s = (s_0 s_1 \cdots s_n s_{n+1} \cdots)$ as close as we desire by repeating sequences of the form

$$\hat{s}_n = (s_0 \cdots s_n s_0 \cdots s_n \cdots).$$

By the lemma, as $n \to \infty$, $\hat{s}_n \to s$. Hence repeating sequences are dense in Σ and it follows that periodic orbits are dense in Λ.

Note also that there is a dense σ-orbit in Σ. For example, the orbit

$$(\underbrace{0\ 1}_{all\ 1\ blocks} \quad \underbrace{00\ 01\ 10\ 11}_{all\ 2\ blocks} \underbrace{000\ 001}_{all\ 3\ blocks} \dots \underbrace{0000}_{all\ 4\ blocks} \dots \dots)$$

comes as close as we wish to any sequence in Σ. Therefore, its preimage under S is a dense orbit in Λ.

We note that F has *sensitive dependence on initial conditions*. By this we mean there exists $\delta > 0$ such that, for any $x \in \Lambda$ and any neighborhood V of x, there exists $y \in V$ and $n > 0$ such that $|F^n(x) - F^n(y)| > \delta$. Indeed, since the itinerary of x and y disagree at some iteration, say the nth, then $F^n(x)$ and $F^n(y)$ lie on opposite sides of A_0. We may therefore choose δ to be the width of A_0.

Finally, we note that $F|\Lambda$ is also *topologically transitive*. A mapping F is topologically transitive if for any pair U, V of open sets, there exists $k \geq 0$ such that $F^k(U) \cap V \neq \varnothing$. That σ has this property is clear: let s and t be two sequences in Σ with $s = (s_0 s_1 s_2 \cdots)$ and $t = (t_0 t_1 t_2 \cdots)$. Let U be a neighborhood of s and V of t. Choose n so that the balls of radius $1/2^n$ about s and t lie in U and V. Then any sequence of the form

$$x = (s_0 \cdots s_n\ t_0 \cdots t_n\ {*}{*}{*} \cdots)$$

lies in U and satisfies $\sigma^{n+1}(x) \in V$.

We remark that the conjugacy S between Λ and Σ allows us to prove the above four facts easily. This is the power of symbolic dynamics.

4. Chaos. Chaos is a much-abused term in dynamical systems. As Phil Holmes has observed, the word has a cataclysmic ring to it, reminiscent of catastrophe theory which suffered so much hyperbole in the early seventies. As Bill Thurston has observed, to call your field "chaos" is an admission of defeat at the outset. Nevertheless, chaotic dynamics has become an important field, not only in mathematics, but also in physics, chemistry, engineering, and other sciences. There is no uniformly accepted definition of chaos in the literature, but that will not hinder us from adopting our own favorite (although perhaps too topological for many people's tastes) definition.

DEFINITION. Let $F : M \to M$ be a map, where M is a metric space. The map F is said to be chaotic if

1. F has sensitive dependence on initial conditions.
2. F is topologically transitive.
3. Periodic points of F are dense in M.

Chaotic maps possess a degree of unpredictability caused by the sensitive dependence on initial conditions: small errors in choosing initial points for orbits may lead to vast errors along the resulting orbits. Chaotic maps also are indecomposable, because by topological transitivity, certain orbits visit the entire space (indeed, one may show easily using the Baire Category Theorem that topological transitivity is equivalent to the existence of a dense orbit). Finally, amidst the unpredictability, there is an element of regularity, namely the periodic points which are dense.

EXAMPLE. As we showed in the previous section, $F(x) = x^2 + c$ is chaotic for $c < c_*$ on the Cantor set Λ.

EXAMPLE. Let S^1 denote the unit circle in the plane and consider the squaring map $S(z) = z^2$ for $|z| = 1$. Then S is chaotic on S^1. To see this, let $U \subset S^1$ be an arc. Then each application of S doubles the arclength of the previous image. Hence there is $n > 0$ such that $S^n(U) \supset S^1$. It follows that S is both topologically transitive and sensitive to initial conditions. Moreover, if $S^n(U)$ contains U in its interior, then there must be a fixed point for S^n in U. This fixed point is clearly repelling.

EXAMPLE. Recall that $F_{-2}(x) = x^2 - 2$ folds the interval $[-2, 2]$ over itself twice. We claim that F_{-2} is chaotic on this interval. To see this, define

$$\phi : S^1 \to [-2, 2]$$

by $\phi(\theta) = 2\cos\theta$. The map ϕ is two-to-one, except at $\theta = 0$ and π. One may check easily that

$$
\begin{array}{ccc}
S^1 & \xrightarrow{\ S\ } & S^1 \\
\downarrow{\scriptstyle \phi} & & \downarrow{\scriptstyle \phi} \\
[-2, 2] & \xrightarrow{\ F_2\ } & [-2, 2]
\end{array}
$$

is a commutative diagram. Thus ϕ maps orbits of S to orbits of F_{-2} (such a ϕ is called a semi-conjugacy). Hence F_{-2} shares all of the dynamical properties of S, and so is chaotic on $[-2, 2]$.

The examples above may be extended to the complex plane. If $z \in \mathbf{C}$ and $|z| \neq 1$, then the behavior of the orbit of z under the squaring map S is quite tame. All orbits tend to ∞ if $|z| > 1$; all orbits tend to 0 if $|z| < 1$. Thus the plane decomposes into two invariant regions, the chaotic set, S^1, and the stable set, the complement of S^1. The chaotic set in complex dynamics has a special name:

DEFINITION. Let $F : \mathbf{C} \to \mathbf{C}$ be complex analytic. The Julia set of F, $J(F)$, is the closure of the set of repelling periodic points for F.

We refer to the contribution of Keen in this volume for more details about the Julia set and its properties.

Note that the semi-conjugacy between S and F_{-2} extends to the complex plane. Define

$$\Phi(z) = 2\cos(-i\log z) = z + \frac{1}{z}.$$

Then we have the commutative diagram:

$$\begin{array}{ccc} \mathbf{C} & \xrightarrow{\;S\;} & \mathbf{C} \\ \Big\downarrow{\scriptstyle\Phi} & & \Big\downarrow{\scriptstyle\Phi} \\ \mathbf{C} & \xrightarrow{\;F_{-2}\;} & \mathbf{C} \end{array}$$

In particular, all orbits except those on the interval $[-2, 2]$ tend to ∞ under iteration of F_{-2}. Since repelling periodic points are dense in $[-2, 2]$, it follows that $J(F_{-2}) = [-2, 2]$.

5. Sarkovskii's Theorem. In this section we discuss a remarkable and surprising theorem due to Sarkovskii. This theorem only holds for one-dimensional dynamical systems, but it is nevertheless remarkable for its lack of hypotheses yet powerful results. We order the real numbers as follows:

$$3 \triangleright 5 \triangleright 7 \triangleright \cdots 2 \cdot 3 \triangleright 2 \cdot 5 \triangleright 2 \cdot 7 \triangleright \cdots \triangleright 2^2 \cdot 3 \triangleright 2^2 \cdot 5 \triangleright \cdots$$

$$\cdots \triangleright 2^3 \cdot 3 \triangleright 2^3 \cdot 5 \triangleright \cdots \triangleright 2^4 \triangleright 2^3 \triangleright 2^2 \triangleright 2 \triangleright 1$$

That is, we list all odd numbers in increasing order first, followed by two times the odds, then four times the odds, etc. At the end of the list, we write the remaining numbers, the powers of 2, in decreasing order. Sarkovskii's theorem states:

THEOREM. *Suppose $F : \mathbf{R} \to \mathbf{R}$ is continuous. If F has a periodic point of period n and $n \triangleright k$ in the above ordering, then F also has a periodic point of period k.*

Let us list some immediate consequences of this result.

COROLLARY. *If F has a periodic point of period 3, then F has periodic points of all periods.*

COROLLARY. *Suppose F has a periodic point whose period is not a power of two. Then F has infinitely many periodic points.*

Note that Sarkovskii's Theorem lends credibility to our statement in §2 about the period-doubling route to chaos. If a continuous map has only finitely many periodic points, then they must have periods $2^0, 2^1, \ldots, 2^N$ for some N. Moreover, as the dynamics of a family of maps increases in complexity by adding new periodic points, then they must appear in a specific order: 2^{N+1} first, then 2^{N+2}, etc. This does not say that the orbits appear in period-doubling bifurcations, but something like that must occur.

We remark that Sarkovskii's Theorem is also sharp. If $n \triangleright k$ in the ordering, there are examples of continuous maps which have cycles of period k but not of period n.

Rather than prove Sarkovskii's Theorem in complete detail, we will prove only the following special case. The proof of the full theorem involves no new ideas but considerably more bookkeeping. See [**D**].

PROPOSITION. *Suppose a continuous map $F : \mathbf{R} \to \mathbf{R}$ has a periodic point of period 3. Then F has periodic points of all periods.*

PROOF. The proof will depend on two elementary observations. First, if I and J are closed intervals with $I \subset J$ and $F(I) \supset J$, then F has a fixed point in I. This is a consequence of the Intermediate Value Theorem. The second observation is the following: suppose $A_0, A_1, \ldots, A_n$ are closed intervals and $F(A_i) \supset A_{i+1}$ for $i = 0, \ldots, n-1$. Then there exists at least one subinterval J_0 of A_0 which is mapped onto A_1. There is a similar subinterval in A_1 which is mapped onto A_2 and thus there is a subinterval $J_1 \subset J_0$ having the property that $F(J_1) \subset A_1$ and $F^2(J_1) = A_2$. Continuing in this fashion, we find a nested sequence of subintervals which map into the various A_i in order.

To prove the proposition, let $a, b, c \in \mathbf{R}$ and suppose $F(a) = b$, $F(b) = c$, and $F(c) = a$. We assume that $a > b > c$. The only other possibility is handled similarly.

Let $I_0 = [a, b]$ and $I_1 = [b, c]$. Our assumptions imply that $F(I_0) \supset I_1$ and $F(I_1) \supset I_0 \cup I_1$. The graph of F thus shows that there is a fixed point between b and c. See Figure 5.1.

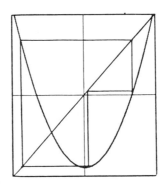

FIGURE 5.1. The graph of F with a period 3 orbit.

Similarly F^2 must have fixed points between a and b and at least one of these points must be a period 2 point. So let us fix $n > 3$ and produce a periodic point of period n.

Inductively, we define a nested sequence of intervals $A_0, A_1, \ldots, A_{n-2} \subset I_1$ as follows. Let $A_0 = I_1$. Since $F(I_1) \supset I_1$, there is a subinterval $A_1 \subset A_0$ such that $F(A_1) = A_0 = I_1$. Continuing, we find a subinterval $A_{n-2} \subset A_{n-3}$ such that $F(A_{n-2}) = A_{n-3}$, $F^2(A_{n-2}) = A_{n-4}, \ldots, F^{n-2}(A_{n-2}) = A_0 = I_1$.

Now since $F(I_1) \supset I_0$, there is a subinterval $A_{n-1} \subset A_{n-2}$ such that $F^{n-1}(A_{n-1}) = I_0$. Finally, since $F(I_0) \supset I_1$, we have $F^n(A_{n-1}) \supset I_1 \supset A_{n-1}$. It follows from our first observation that F^n has a fixed point in A_{n-1}. We claim that this point actually has period n for F. This follows since $F^i(A_{n-1}) \subset I_1$ for $i = 0, \ldots, n-2$. But $F^{n-1}(A_{n-1}) \subset I_0$ while $F^n(A_n) \supset I_1$.

So this point has its first $n - 2$ iterates in I_1, then it hops to I_0, and then back to I_1. This completes the proof.

q.e.d.

With this result, it is illuminating to investigate a specific example. Let $F(z) = z^2 + c$ where $c = -1.755$. Using a computer, it is easy to check that there is an attracting periodic orbit of period 3 which, to four decimal places, is given by

$$0 \to -1.755 \to 1.325 \to 0.$$

If one inputs virtually any number into the computer and computes its orbit, then one finds that the orbit is attracted to the periodic orbit above. Sarkovskii's Theorem, however, asserts that there must be infinitely many distinct periodic points for F. Where are they? Actually, these orbits are hard to find because they are all repelling periodic points. One does not in general "see" repelling points on a computer.

This brings up several questions. Why, of all the infinitely many periodic points for F, is only one attracting? There is a deep answer to this question: for complex analytic maps, each attracting orbit must attract at least one critical point for the map. See the contribution of Keen in this volume for more details on this. Since our map has only one critical point, at 0, there can be at most one attracting periodic orbit.

A second question involves symbolic dynamics. Can we use symbolic dynamics to study the dynamical behavior of this map? The answer is yes, and here is a sketch of how to proceed. Let us find (using a computer) three open sets, $\mathcal{O}_1$ about 0, $\mathcal{O}_2$ about -1.755, and $\mathcal{O}_3$ about 1.325. The $\mathcal{O}_i$ are to be chosen so that $\overline{F^3(\mathcal{O}_i)} \subset \mathcal{O}_i$ and $F(\mathcal{O}_i) \subset \mathcal{O}_{i+1}$. This can always be done. Now let I_0 denote the closed interval between $\mathcal{O}_1$ and $\mathcal{O}_3$ and let I_1 be the closed interval between $\mathcal{O}_2$ and $\mathcal{O}_1$. See Figure 5.2.

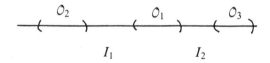

FIGURE 5.2. The open intervals $\mathcal{O}_i$.

We may choose the $\mathcal{O}_i$ so that $|(F^3)'(x)| > 1$ on $I_0 \cup I_1$. Then note the following

$$F(I_0) \supset I_1,$$
$$F(I_1) \supset I_0 \cup I_1,$$

and, in each case, the interval in question is stretched over its image.

We may now introduce symbolic dynamics as follows. Let

$$\Lambda = \{x \mid F^n(x) \in I_0 \cup I_1 \text{ all } n \geq 0\}$$

as before. Λ is a Cantor set. What are the dynamics on Λ? We introduce a new model space for the dynamics on Λ. Let Σ' denote the set of all sequences $(s_0 s_1 s_2 \cdots)$ consisting of 0's and 1's and having the special property that if $s_j = 0$ then $s_{j+1} = 1$. That is, each sequence in Σ' has no adjacent pair of 0's. If we define the itinerary map

$$S : \Lambda \rightarrow \Sigma'$$

as before, then we see that $F(I_0) \supset I_1$ forces this condition on Σ'. The diagram

$$
\begin{array}{ccc}
\Lambda & \xrightarrow{\ F\ } & \Lambda \\
{\scriptstyle S}\downarrow & & \downarrow{\scriptstyle S} \\
\Sigma' & \xrightarrow{\ \sigma\ } & \Sigma'
\end{array}
$$

is easily seen to commute, so the shift map on Σ' provides the model for the dynamics on Λ.

We immediately see lots of periodic points for σ in Σ'. Indeed, the repeating sequence

$$(0\underbrace{1\ldots1}_{n-1}0\underbrace{1\ldots1}_{n-1}\ldots)$$

corresponds to an orbit of period n in Λ. Incidentally, the reader will note that this is precisely the orbit constructed above in our proof of the special case of Sarkovskii's Theorem.

The pair (Σ', σ) is called a subshift of finite type. It is easy to check that F is chaotic on Λ by verifying this on the subshift.

6. An experiment. Many of the topics discussed in this paper and, indeed, in the rest of this book come together naturally in the study of Julia sets of complex analytic maps. Fractals, chaos, bifurcations, Hausdorff dimension— all of these are essential ingredients in the study of the dynamics of complex analytic maps, as is shown nicely in the contributions of Keen and Branner in this volume. In this section, we mention an analogous theory for the iteration of entire (rather than rational) functions. Because of the presence of the essential singularity at ∞, these maps possess a tremendous amount of chaotic behavior.

Consider, for example, the family of complex exponential functions given by $\lambda \exp z$ for $\lambda \in \mathbf{R}$. It is known that the Julia set for these functions is the closure of the set of points whose orbits tend to ∞. The rough reason for this is, as we mentioned above, the essential singularity at ∞. Recall that, by Picard's Theorem, any neighborhood of ∞ is mapped infinitely often over the entire plane minus at most two points (which are, of course, 0 and ∞). This means that orbits which come close to ∞ experience a tremendous amount of sensitive dependence. To be precise, this only occurs in certain regions near ∞, namely in the right half-plane Re $z >$ some large constant. This suggests a way to plot experimentally the Julia set of the exponential function. For a set of points in a grid in the complex plane, we will compute the orbit of each point and check to see if this orbit "comes close to ∞". If it does, we will color the initial point with a color that indicates how quickly the orbit goes to ∞. Red and orange shades indicate that the orbit of the initial point tends to ∞ quickly; yellow and green shades indicate a moderate number of iterations; and blue and violet shades indicate that a large number of iterations are necessary before the orbit gets too large. What do we mean by "goes to ∞?" The condition we use is that some point on the orbit has real part larger than 50. The reason for this is that e^{50} is quite large, and besides, one may rigorously prove that, if some point on the orbit enters this region, then there is a point in the Julia set very close to the starting value.

The results of this experiment are shown in Color Plates 1 and 2. Color Plate 1 depicts the Julia set of the function $.36e^z$ and Color Plate 2 depicts the Julia set of $.37e^z$. One may check that the Julia set of any exponential of the form λe^z with $\lambda < 1/e$ looks essentially the same as Color Plate 1, whereas when $\lambda > 1/e$, the Julia set of λe^z seems to explode. In fact, this is completely true: when $\lambda < 1/e$, the Julia set is a nowhere dense subset of the half-plane Re $z > 1$. But when $\lambda > 1/e$, the Julia set suddenly becomes the whole complex plane. That is, the chaotic set has suddenly exploded! See [D1,2] for more details on this.

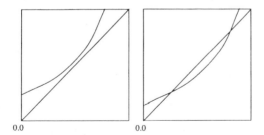

FIGURE 6.1. The graphs of λe^z for a. $\lambda < 1/e$ and b. $\lambda > 1/e$.

What causes this bifurcation? Actually, this rather large global bifurcation is a consequence of a simple saddle-node bifurcation. In Figure 6.1 we have displayed the graphs of the complex exponential function λe^z in two cases: $\lambda < 1/e$ and $\lambda > 1/e$. Note that in the latter case all orbits on the real line escape, whereas, in the former case, many of the orbits tend to the attracting fixed point which appears as the parameter decreases below $1/e$. According to our discussion above, the real line is in the Julia set in the former case, while only the half line to the right of the repelling fixed point is in the Julia set when $\lambda < 1/e$.

We should remark that not all points in the Julia set escape under iteration; remember, the Julia set is the *closure* of the set of escaping orbits. As in Keen's paper, the Julia set is also the closure of the set of repelling periodic points. Thus there are repelling periodic points arbitrarily close to any escaping point, and vice versa.

The exact structure of the Julia set of transcendental functions like the exponential is known: when the Julia set is not the whole plane, it is a "Cantor bouquet". By this we mean that the Julia set is a Cantor set of curves, each of which is homeomorphic to $[0, \infty)$ and each of which extends to ∞ in the right half-plane. It is known that, in this case, the Lebesgue measure of the Julia set is zero but its Hausdorff dimension is two! See [**Mc**]. Bifurcations such as the one above occur in a variety of entire transcendental functions. For example, in Color Plates 3 and 4 we display the Julia sets of $.66i \cos z$ and $.68i \cos z$. Again one sees that the Julia set explodes as the parameter $i\lambda$ increases through $.67\ldots$, and again it is a saddle-node bifurcation that leads to this explosion. We remark that, unlike the exponential function, the Julia set for any member of the family $\lambda \cos z$ has infinite Lebesgue measure. This accounts for the fact that the colored region in Color Plate 3 seems to occupy a larger area than that of Color Plate 1, even though both Julia sets are Cantor bouquets.

REFERENCES

[**A**] V. I. Arnol'd, *Ordinary differential equations,* M. I. T. Press, Cambridge, Mass., 1973.

[**AS**] R. Abraham and C. Shaw, *Dynamics: The geometry of behavior,* Aerial Press, Santa Cruz, Calif., 1982.

[**CE**] P. Collet and J.-P. Eckmann, *Iterated maps of the interval as dynamical systems,* Birkhäuser, Boston, 1980.

[**D**] R. L. Devaney, *An introduction to chaotic dynamical systems,* Addison-Wesley, Menlo Park, 1985.

[**D1**] ____, *Bursts into chaos,* Phys. Lett. **104** (1984), 385-387.

[**D2**] ____, *Chaotic bursts in nonlinear dynamical systems,* Science **235** (1987), 342-345.

[**F**] M. Feigenbaum, *Quantitative universality for a class of nonlinear transformations,* J. Statist. Phys. **19** (1978), 25-52.

[**GH**] J. Guckenheimer and P. Holmes, *Nonlinear oscillations, dynamical systems, and bifurcation of vector fields,* Springer-Verlag, New York, 1983.

[**HS**] M. Hirsch and S. Smale, *Differential equations, dynamical systems, and linear algebra,* Academic Press, New York, 1974.

[**M**] B. Mandelbrot, *The fractal geometry of nature,* Freeman, San Francisco, 1982.

[**Mc**] C. McMullen, *Area and Hausdorff dimension of Julia sets of entire functions,* Trans. Amer. Math. Soc. **300** (1987), 329-342.

[**PdM**] J. Palis and W. de Melo, *Geometric theory of dynamical systems,* Springer-Verlag, New York, 1982.

[**PR**] H.-O. Peitgen and P. Richter, *The beauty of fractals,* Springer-Verlag, New York, 1986.

[**S**] M. Shub, *Global stability of dynamical systems,* Springer-Verlag, New York, 1986.

DEPARTMENT OF MATHEMATICS, BOSTON UNIVERSITY, BOSTON, MASSACHUSETTS 02215

Proceedings of Symposia in Applied Mathematics
Volume 39, 1989

Nonlinear Oscillations
and the Smale Horseshoe Map

PHILIP HOLMES

ABSTRACT. This paper introduces, via an example, some basic ideas in the global analysis of dynamical systems. In particular, we indicate how it may be proved that Smale's horseshoe map is contained in the Poincaré map of the simple pendulum subject to periodically varying torque. We indicate the remarkable physical consequences which result.

0. Introduction. In this article we introduce some important ideas in the global theory of dynamical systems by means of a simple example: the pendulum subject to a small oscillating torque and weak dissipation. We use the second order ordinary differential equation describing this system to introduce such ideas as the Poincaré map, Smale's horseshoe map and the chaos that accompanies it, and the Melnikov perturbation method, with which one goes hunting for horseshoes. It would be imprudent to attempt, and impossible to succeed in, a comprehensive tutorial on dynamical systems within either the confines of this article or the hour of speech and gesture granted us by the organizers. For those with a year or two of interrupted leisure, the books by Arnold [**1973**], Andronov et. al. [**1966**] or Hirsch-Smale [**1974**] provide good introductory material, while those of Arnold [**1982**], Palis-de Melo [**1982**], Irwin [**1980**] and (succumbing to chauvinism) Guckenheimer-Holmes [**1983**] contain more advanced material. Some aspects of the present treatment are adapted from the latter book.

In the following sections we introduce our model problem and describe the Poincaré map §1. We then discuss some general features of iterated (invertible) maps on the plane §2, before introducing and describing Smale's horseshoe map §3. We return to our example and describe the Melnikov perturbation calculation in §4, and finally summarize the fruits of our labours in §5. It is worth noting that Smale invented the horseshoe map while attempting to understand the papers of Cartwright-Littlewood [**1945**] and Levinson [**1949**] on the periodically forced Van der Pol oscillator (cf. Smale [**1963**,

1980 *Mathematics Subject Classification* (1985 *Revision*). Primary 58F99.

1967]: the story is told nicely in Smale [**1980**]). As in that case, specific examples have often led the way to general ideas in dynamical systems theory. It is therefore entirely appropriate that we should start with a (deceptively) simple model problem.

1. The pendulum equation. Consider the simple pendulum of Figure 1. A point mass m is suspended by a rigid, massless rod of length l pivoted freely at 0 to swing in a plane. Three forces act on the bob: gravitation ($-mg$, vertically), friction or dissipation due to air resistance ($-cv$, tangentially), and the external time varying torque $\delta T(t)$ applied at the pivot. The minus signs are conventional, reflecting that the forces oppose motion as indicated, and friction is modelled by the simplest possible law: resistance is linearly proportional to speed. The state of the system is uniquely specified by the pair $(\theta, \frac{d\theta}{dt})$, angular position and velocity. Resolving the forces in the tangential direction, and appealing to Newton's famous second law (force = mass×acceleration), we obtain the second order ordinary differential equation

$$(1.1) \qquad \delta l T(t) - cl\frac{d\theta}{dt} - mg \sin\theta = m\frac{d}{dt}\left(l\frac{d\theta}{dt}\right).$$

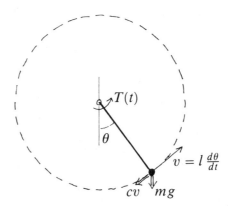

FIGURE 1. The simple pendulum subject to torque and friction.

A slight rearrangement of terms and a change of time scale yields the system we shall study:

$$(1.2) \qquad \ddot{\theta} + \sin\theta = \delta S(t) - \gamma\dot{\theta},$$

where $(\dot{\ }) = \frac{d}{dt}(\ )$ (t is the new time), $S(t) = \frac{l}{gm}T(t)$ and $\gamma = \frac{c}{m}\sqrt{\frac{g}{l}}$.

When the parameters δ, γ are equal to zero we have the classical pendulum: this equation can be solved in closed form using elliptic functions, since solutions simply run around on level sets of the hamiltonian energy function

$$(1.3) \qquad\qquad H(\theta, \dot{\theta}) = \frac{\dot{\theta}^2}{2} + (1 - \cos\theta)$$

(= kinetic + potential energy). In §4 we shall exploit this to approximate solutions of the *perturbed* problem for small δ, $\gamma \neq 0$.

Before introducing the Poincaré map, we rewrite (1.2) as a system of first order differential equations. We let $\dot{\theta} = v$ and treat time as a (trivially evolving) third dependent variable:

$$\dot{\theta} = v,$$
$$(1.4) \qquad\qquad \dot{v} = -\sin\theta + \delta S(t) - \gamma v,$$
$$\dot{t} = 1.$$

At this point we make the additional assumption that $S(t)$ is periodic of period T (e.g. $S(t) = \cos wt$, $T = 2\pi/w$): the *phase-space* or *state-space* of (1.4) is then $(\theta, v, t) \in S^1 \times \mathbf{R} \times S^1 \overset{\text{def}}{=} M$, since the state of the system depends only on the angle θ (not the total number of turns the pendulum has executed) and the phase $t \bmod T$ of the forcing function $S(t)$ (as well as the velocity $v = \dot{\theta}$). There is already some nontrivial topology in this simple example!

We next define a *cross section* $\Sigma = \{(\theta, s, t) | t = 0\} \subset M$ which solutions pierce transversely, in view of the third component $\dot{t} = 1$ of (1.4). The Poincaré map $P: \Sigma \to \Sigma$ is defined by picking a point $(\theta_0, v_0) \in \Sigma$ and integrating the equation (1.4) to find the point at which the solution based at (θ_0, v_0) next intersects Σ after time T has elapsed. Thus we have

$$(1.5) \qquad\qquad P(\theta_0, v_0) = (\theta(T; \theta_0, v_0), v(T; \theta_0, v_0)),$$

where $\theta(t; \theta_0, v_0)$, $v(t; \theta_0, v_0)$ $(t = t)$ is the solution to (1.4) based at (θ_0, v_0). In Figure 2 we sketch the construction for the unperturbed pendulum equation $(\delta = \gamma = 0)$: note that the level *curves* of the Hamiltonian (1.3) become *sheets* in the three-dimensional (suspended) phase space M. Also, the *periodic orbits* $(\theta, v) = (0, 0)$ and $(\pi, 0)$ correspond to *fixed points* for the map P (the latter are marked γ on Figure 2(b)). In the unperturbed case the periodic orbits are trivial, so θ and v do not change with time. For $\delta \neq 0$, on a T-periodic orbit θ and v do vary as t moves from 0 to T, but it should be intuitively clear that P will still have a fixed point. Similarly, a kt-periodic orbit or *subharmonic* corresponds to a k-periodic *cycle* for P.

We end this section by remarking that it is a nice exercise to show that the existence-uniqueness theorem for ODEs implies that P is a diffeomorphism and that, for systems with linear damping like (1.4), the Jacobian derivative DP of P satisfies

$$(1.6) \qquad\qquad \det(DP) = e^{-\gamma T}.$$

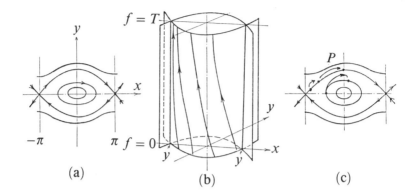

FIGURE 2. Phase plane (a), flow in extended phase space (b), and Poincaré map (c) for the unperturbed pendulum (identify $x = -\pi$ and $x = \pi$ so that (x, y) space is the cylinder (or annulus)).

2. Some basic facts about maps. We now turn to a brief review of maps, concentrating on the two-dimensional case, although everything generalizes to n dimensions. Devaney's contribution to this volume contains a good discussion of the one-dimensional case and his book (Devaney [1986] has additional two-dimensional information).

Let $P: \mathbf{R}^2 \to \mathbf{R}^2$ be a (smooth) map and p a fixed point ($p = P(p)$). We call the linear system

$$(2.1) \qquad\qquad x \mapsto DP(p)x$$

the *linearization* of P at p. $DP(p)$ is a 2×2 matrix: denote its eigenvalues λ_1, λ_2. By arguments similar to those in Devaney's article, one easily sees that p is stable if both eigenvalues of $DP(p)$ lie within the unit circle ($|\lambda_j| < 1$: $j = 1, 2$). If this is the case we call p a *sink*. When $|\lambda_1| < 1 < |\lambda_2|$ p is an (unstable) *saddle point* and when $|\lambda_j| > 1$, $j = 1, 2$, p is a *source*. If $|\lambda_j| \neq 1$, $j = 1, 2$, we call p *hyperbolic* and the Hartman-Grobman theorem (cf. Devaney [1986], Guckenheimer-Holmes [1983]) guarantees that the dynamical behavior of the linearization (2.1) holds in a neighborhood U of p for the fully nonlinear map F.

For our unperturbed example the fixed point(s) $(\theta, v) = (\pm\pi, 0)$ of the map $P = P_0$ are clearly saddle points. In fact the linearized map can be obtained by integrating the linearized differential equation linearized at $(\theta, v) = (\pm\pi, 0)$:

$$(2.2) \qquad \begin{aligned} \dot{\xi}_1 &= \xi_2, \\ \dot{\xi}_2 &= -\cos(\pm\pi)\xi_1 = \xi_1. \end{aligned}$$

Elementary analysis shows that the fundamental solution matrix to this system may be written

$$(2.3) \qquad \begin{bmatrix} \cosh t & \sinh t \\ \sinh t & \cosh t \end{bmatrix}$$

and hence that the time T map, which gives DP_0, is

$$(2.4.) \qquad DP_0(\pm\pi, 0) \cdot \xi = \begin{bmatrix} \cosh T & \sinh T \\ \sinh T & \cosh T \end{bmatrix} \begin{pmatrix} \xi_1 \\ \xi_2 \end{pmatrix}.$$

The matrix DP_0 has eigenvalues

$$(2.5) \qquad \lambda_{1,2} = \cosh T \pm \sinh T = e^T, e^{-T},$$

and since $e^{-T} < 1 < e^T$, the point(s) $(\pm\pi, 0)$ are, as expected, saddle points. Actually, since θ is measured modulo 2π, and both equilibria correspond to the pendulum standing straight up (Figure 1), these points are identified in M.

It is reasonable to believe, and possible to prove by a simple application of the implicit function theorem, that, for small δ, $\gamma = \mathscr{O}(\varepsilon)$, P_0 perturbs to a nearby map $P_\varepsilon = P_0 + \mathscr{O}(\varepsilon)$, which has a fixed point $P_\varepsilon = (\pi, 0) + \mathscr{O}(\varepsilon)$ with eigenvalues $e^T + \mathscr{O}(\varepsilon)$, $e^{-T} + \mathscr{O}(\varepsilon)$. We use this fact in our perturbation calculations in §4.

The linear system (2.1) can be put into a convenient form by a suitable similarity transformation. In particular, if the eigenvalues are $|\lambda_1| < 1 < |\lambda_2|$, DP may be diagonalized, so that the linear map uncoupled

$$(2.6) \qquad u \mapsto \lambda_1 u, \qquad v \mapsto \lambda_2 v$$

and the two axes $v = 0$, $u = 0$ are then the invariant *stable* and *unstable* *subspaces*, E^s, E^u (Figure 3(a)). The stable manifold theorem (cf. Guckenheimer-Holmes [1983], Devaney [1986]) asserts that, locally, the structure for the nonlinear system

$$(2.7) \qquad x \mapsto P(x)$$

is qualitatively similar. More precisely, in a neighborhood U of p there exist *local* stable and unstable manifolds $W^s_{\text{loc}}(p)$, $W^u_{\text{loc}}(p)$, tangent to E^s, E^u at p, and as smooth as P. By taking backward and forward images of arcs contained in these manifolds one constructs the *global* stable and unstable manifolds.

$$(2.8) \qquad W^s(p) = \bigcup_{n\geq 0} P^{-n}(W^s_{\text{loc}}(p)), \qquad W^u(p) = \bigcup_{n\geq 0} P^n(W^u_{\text{loc}}(p)),$$

which contain all points $x \in \mathbf{R}^2$ which are forward (resp. backward) asymptotic to p under iteration of P.

While the local structure is nice, the global structure need not be, and herein lies much of the reason for "chaotic motions," as we shall see. We call a point $q \in W^u(p) \cap W^s(p)$ a *homoclinic point*, following the terminology of Poincaré [1899]. By definition, the orbit $\{P^n(q)\}_{n=-\infty}^{\infty}$ of q is both

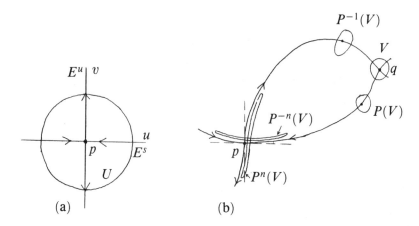

FIGURE 3. (a) Invariant subspaces for linear map; (b) Invariant manifolds for nonlinear map, showing a homoclinic point, q.

forward and backward asymptotic to p. If the manifolds $W^s(p)$, $W^u(p)$ intersect transversely at q, then iteration of a small region V containing q causes $P^n(V)$ and $P^{-n}(V)$ to "pile up" on $W^u(p)$, $W^s(p)$ respectively as $n \mapsto \infty$ (Figure 3(b)). (That this occurs in the controlled fashion of C^1-convergence of transversals to W^u, W^s at q is the content of the Lambda Lemma; Newhouse [1980], Guckenheimer-Holmes [1983].) In such a situation the Smale-Birkhoff homoclinic theorem, described in the next section, shows that V and its images contain a very complicated invariant set for P.

We end by noting that, for the unperturbed pendulum Poincaré map of Figure 2(c), all points on the level sets

(2.9) $$H(\theta, v) = \frac{v^2}{2} + (1 - \cos\theta) = 0$$

are homoclinic to the point $(-\pi, 0) = (\pi, 0)$. However, these points are all nontransversal, since in this very special case the two manifolds are identical. Perturbation of this degenerate structure to produce transversal homoclinic points is treated in §4.

3. Smale's horseshoe map. As Poincaré [1890] realized, the presence of homoclinic points can vastly complicate dynamical behavior. However, the very fact that their existence implies recurrent motions makes the situation amenable to at least a partial analysis. Consider the effect of the map P of Figure 3(b), containing a transverse homoclinic point q to a hyperbolic saddle p, on a "rectangular" strip S containing p and q in its boundary. As n increases, $P^n(S)$ is contracted horizontally and expanded vertically until the image $P^N(S)$ loops around and intersects S and P in a 'horseshoe' shape

(Figure 4). To prove that the rates of contraction and expansion are uniformly bounded, one shrinks the width of S until many iterates occur for
which $P^j(S)$ lies in a neighborhood U of p and the dynamics is therefore
dominated by the linear map $DP(p)$ (cf. (2.6)).

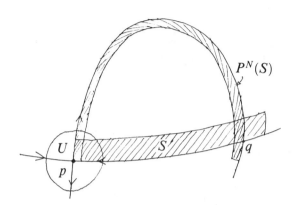

FIGURE 4. P^N has a horseshoe.

A simple model for this situation was provided by Smale [1963], who
introduced the map $F: S \mapsto \mathbf{R}^2$ of the square $[0, 1] \times [0, 1] \subset \mathbf{R}^2$ sketched in
Figure 5(a). The map is linear on the two horizontal strips H_i whose images
are the vertical strips V_i, $i = 0, 1$; the linearizations being

$$(3.1) \qquad DF(x)|_{x \in H_1} = \begin{bmatrix} \lambda & 0 \\ 0 & \gamma \end{bmatrix}, \qquad DF(x)|_{x \in H_2} = \begin{bmatrix} -\lambda & 0 \\ 0 & -\gamma \end{bmatrix},$$

with $0 < \lambda < 1 < \gamma$. Thus $F|_{H_i}$ contracts horizontally and expands vertically
in a uniform manner. Smale studied the structure of the set of points Λ
which never leave S under iteration of F. By definition $\Lambda = \bigcap_{n=-\infty}^{\infty} F^n(S)$:
the intersection of all images and preimages of S. Now $F^{-1}(S) \cap S = H_1 \cup H_2$
and $S \cap F(S) = V_1 \cup V_2$ so $F^n(S)$ is the union of four rectangles of height γ^{-1}
and width λ (Figure 5(a)). Similarly $\bigcap_{n=-2}^{2} F^n(S)$ is the union of 16 rectangles
of height γ^{-2} and width λ^2, $\bigcap_{n=-k}^{k} F^n(S)$ is the union of 2^{2k} rectangles and,
passing to the limit, Λ turns out to be a *Cantor set*: an uncountable point set,
every member of which is a limit point.

To see this more easily, consider the set of points which never leave $I =
[0, 1] \subset R$ under iteration of the one-dimensional map f of Figure 5(b). After
one iterate the 'middle' interval I_c is lost, after two iterates its preimages I_{0c},
I_{1c} are lost, etc. Removing middle intervals of fixed proportional size (α, say)
produces the classic 'middle α' Cantor set Λ', the one-dimensional analogue
of Λ. We remark that the map f is qualitatively like the famous quadratic
map $x \mapsto ax(1-x)$ or $x \mapsto c - x^2$ (cf. the article by Devaney in this volume).

The sets Λ and Λ' can be coded in a way which describes their dynamics.
To each $x \in \Lambda$ we assign a bi-infinite sequence $\phi(x) = \{\phi_j(x)\}_{j=-\infty}^{\infty}$ of

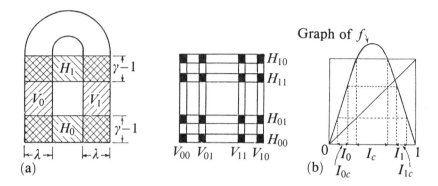

FIGURE 5. (a) The two-dimensional horseshoe and (b)
its one-dimensional analogue.

the symbols 0, 1 by the rule $\phi_j(x) = i$ if $F^j(x) \in H_i$ $(i = 0, 1)$. Thus $\phi_j(F(x)) = \phi_{j+1}(x)$ and the action of F on Λ corresponds to the action of the shift σ on the space of symbol sequences Σ. Moreover, every symbol sequence corresponds to an orbit realized by F, since the images V_i lie fully across their preimages H_i. In fact that map $\phi\colon \Lambda \mapsto \Sigma$ is a homeomorphism and the diagram

$$
\begin{array}{ccc}
\Lambda & \xrightarrow{\ F\ } & \Lambda \\
\downarrow{\scriptstyle\phi} & & \downarrow{\scriptstyle\phi} \\
\Sigma & \xrightarrow{\ \sigma\ } & \Sigma
\end{array}
$$

commutes. We say that $F|\Lambda$ is *topologically conjugate to a (full) shift on two symbols.* For $x \in \Lambda'$ one does the same but using only semi-infinite (positive going) sequences since f is noninvertible. More details can be found in Devaney's article. The main advantage of this method of symbolic dynamics is that one can study the orbits of $F|_\Lambda$ (or $f|_{\Lambda'}$) combinatorially, by examining symbol sequences. For instance, the 'constant' periodic sequences $\dots 000 \dots \overset{\text{def}}{=} (0)'$ and $\dots 111 \dots = (1)'$ correspond to fixed points; $(01')$, $(001)'$, $(011)'$, $(0001)'$, etc. to orbits of periods $2, 3, 3, 4$, etc. (here $(\ )'$ denotes periodic extension). In this way one proves the following.

PROPOSITION. *The invariant set Λ of the horseshoe contains: (1) a countable infinity of periodic orbits, including orbits of arbitrarily high period ($\simeq 2^k/k$ orbits of each period k): (2) an uncountable infinity of nonperiodic orbits, including countably many homoclinic and heteroclinic orbits, and (3) a dense orbit.*

Since $F|_{H_1 \cup H_2}$ contracts uniformly by λ horizontally and expands by γ vertically, the eigenvalues $\mu_{1,2}$ of DF^k for any k-periodic orbit satisfy $|\mu_1| = \lambda^k < 1 < |\mu_2| = \gamma^k$ and thus all such orbits are (unstable) saddles. In fact all orbits in Λ have associated with them exponentially strong unstable manifolds and thus almost all pair of points Λ separate exponentially fast under F^n. This *sensitive dependence on initial conditions* leads to what we popularly call "chaos". More strikingly, since *every* bi-infinite sequence in Σ corresponds to an orbit of $F|_\Lambda$, there are uncountably many orbits which behave in a manner indistinguishable from the outcome of repeated tossing of a coin: a quintessentially random process.

Perhaps most important is the fact that Λ is a *structurally stable* set; small perturbations $\tilde{F}$ of F possess a topologically equivalent set $\tilde{\Lambda} \sim \Lambda$. In fact to prove the existence of such sets one does not need linearity of F or f, as in Smale's example; it is sufficient to establish uniform bounds on contraction and expansion. See Moser [1973] and Guckenheimer and Holmes [1983] for more details.

The constructions we have sketched above and in Figure 4 lead one to the fundamental

SMALE-BIRKHOFF HOMOCLINIC THEOREM. *Let* $P: \mathbf{R}^2 \mapsto \mathbf{R}^2$ *be a diffeomorphism possessing a transversal homoclinic point q to a hyperbolic saddle point p. Then, for some $N < \infty$, P has a hyperbolic invariant set Λ on which the Nth iterate P^N is topologically conjugate to a shift on two symbols.*

Birkhoff [1927] had already proved the existence of countably many periodic points in any neighborhood of a homoclinic point, but Smale's construction provided a more complete picture and he extended it to $\mathbf{R}^n$. Infinite dimensional versions of the theorem are also available.

4. Melnikov's perturbation method. Although Smale constructed the horseshoe in connection with a periodically forced oscillator problem it was not until the work of Melnikov [1963] that a general method existed for proving that horseshoes exist in specific Poincaré maps. Tantalizing hints of this technique can be found in Poincaré's [1890] paper on the three body problem and Arnold [1964] applied the idea to Hamiltonian systems around the same time as Melnikov. Thus, as Jerry Marsden has remarked, the method should probably be called the Poincaré-Arnold-Melnikov method. What one actually does is prove that a suitably perturbed, almost Hamiltonian system has a transversal homoclinic orbit and then apply the Smale-Birkhoff homoclinic theorem.

We only outline the simplest version of the method here. See Holmes-Marsden [1981, 1982a, b, 1983] and Wiggins [1988] for extensions to many (even infinitely many) dimensions. Consider a planar ordinary differential equation subject to a small time-periodic perturbation:

$$(4.1) \qquad \dot{x} = f(x) + \varepsilon g(x,t), \qquad g(x,t) = g(x,t+T), \quad x \in \mathbf{R}^2.$$

We suppose that f and g are sufficiently smooth and bounded on bounded sets and that the unperturbed system is Hamiltonian, i.e. there exists a function $H(x) \colon \mathbf{R}^2 \mapsto \mathbf{R}$ such that

(4.2)
$$\dot{x}_1 = f_1(x_1, x_2) = \frac{\partial H}{\partial x_2}(x_1, x_2),$$
$$\dot{x}_2 = f_1(x_1, x_2) = \frac{-\partial H}{\partial x_1}(x_1, x_2).$$

We assume that this unperturbed vector field contains a hyperbolic saddle point p_0 lying in a closed level set of H: thus there is a (degenerate, nontransversal) loop of homoclinic points: Figure 6(a). The orbits on this loop are denoted $x = x_0(t - t_0)$, where t_0 denotes a shift in the initial condition or base point. For precise technical hypothesis see Guckenheimer-Holmes [**1983**, §4.5].

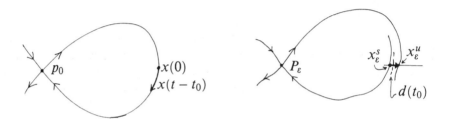

FIGURE 6. (a) The unperturbed loop; (b) The perturbed Poincaré map.

As in §2, we consider the unperturbed and perturbed Poincaré maps P_0, P_ε corresponding to (4.1) with $\varepsilon = 0$ and $\varepsilon \neq 0$. Implicit function arguments show that the hyperbolic fixed point p_0 of p_0 perturbs to a nearby hyperbolic fixed point $p_\varepsilon = p_0 + \mathcal{O}(\varepsilon)$ for P_ε and its stable and unstable manifolds remain close, as indicated in the sketch of Figure 6(b). In fact one proves that the power series representations of solutions $x_\varepsilon^{s,u}$ lying in the perturbed stable and unstable manifolds of the small periodic orbit $\gamma_\varepsilon = p_0 + \mathcal{O}(\varepsilon)$ of (4.1; $\varepsilon \neq 0$) are valid in the following *semi-infinite* time intervals:

(4.3)
$$x_\varepsilon^s(t, t_0) = x_0(t - t_0) + \varepsilon x_1^s(t, t_0) + \mathcal{O}(\varepsilon^2), \qquad t \in [t_0, \infty);$$
$$x_\varepsilon^u(t, t_0) = x_0(t - t_0) + \varepsilon x_1^u(t, t_0) + \mathcal{O}(\varepsilon^2), \qquad t \in (-\infty, t_0].$$

This follows from the usual finite time Gronwall estimates and the fact that these special solutions are "trapped" in the local stable and unstable manifolds and thus have well controlled asymptotic behavior as $|t| \mapsto \infty$. One can therefore seek the leading order terms $x_1^{s,u}(t, t_0)$ as solutions of the first variational equation obtained by substituting (4.3) into (4.1) and expanding in powers of ε:

(4.4)
$$\dot{x}_1^{s,u} = Df(x_0(t - t_0))x_1^{s,u} + g(x_0(t - t_0), t).$$

Now, while equation (4.4) is linear, it is usually very hard to solve, since $Df(x_0(t - t_0))$ is a time varying 2×2 matrix and is not even periodic. Here the idea of Melnikov comes to our rescue. He realized that, to estimate the distance $d(t_0)$ between the perturbed stable and unstable manifolds at a base point t_0 of the unperturbed solution, one need not solve (4.4) explicitly. His method goes as follows.

From (4.3) and Figure 6(b), we have

$$d(t_0) = x_\varepsilon^u(t_0, t_0) - x_\varepsilon^s(t_0, t_0)$$

$$(4.5) \qquad = \frac{\varepsilon(x_1^u(t_0, t_0) - x_1^s(t_0, t_0)) \cdot f^\perp(x_0(0))}{\|f(x_0(0))\|} + \mathscr{O}(\varepsilon)^2,$$

where $f^\perp(x_0(0))$ denotes the normal to the unperturbed solution vector $f(x_0(0))$. Since $a \cdot b^\perp = b \times a$ for vectors in $\mathbf{R}^2$, we can rewrite (4.5) as

$$d(t_0) = \varepsilon \frac{f(x_0(0)) \times (x_1^u(t_0, t_0)) - x_1^s(t_0, t_0)}{\|f(x_0(0))\|} + \mathscr{O}(\varepsilon^2)$$

$$(4.6) \qquad \overset{\text{def}}{=} \varepsilon \frac{\Delta^u(t_0, t_0) - \Delta^s(t_0, t_0)}{\|f(x_0(0))\|} + \mathscr{O}(\varepsilon^2).$$

If the quantity $\Delta^u - \Delta^s$ has simple zeros as t_0 varies it follows from the implicit function theorem that, for $\varepsilon \neq 0$ small enough, the distance $d(t_0)$ changes sign as t_0 varies and consequently that the perturbed manifolds intersect transversely. To compute $\Delta^u - \Delta^s$ we introduce time varying functions

$$\Delta^{u,s}(t, t_0) = f(x_0(t - t_0)) \times x_1^{u,s}(t, t_0)$$

and compute

$$\dot{\Delta}^s = Df(x_0)\dot{x}_0 \times x_1^s + f(x_0) \times \dot{x}_1^s$$
$$= Df(x_0)f(x_0) \times x_1^s + f(x_0) \times [Df(x_0)x_1^s + g(x_0, t)]$$
$$= \text{trace}\, Df(x_0)f(x_0) \times x_1^s + f(x_0) \times g(x_0, t)$$
$$(4.7) \qquad = f(x_0(t - t_0)) \times g(x_0(t - t_0), t).$$

Here we substitute for $\dot{x}_1^s$ from (4.4) and use $\dot{x}_0 = f(x_0)$, a matrix-cross product identity, and finally appeal to the fact that

$$(4.8) \qquad \text{trace}\, Df = \frac{\partial f_1}{\partial x_1} + \frac{\partial f_2}{\partial x_2} = \frac{\partial^2 H}{\partial x_1 \partial x_2} - \frac{\partial^2 H}{\partial x_2 \partial x_1} \equiv 0,$$

since f is Hamiltonian. Integrating (4.7) we have

$$\Delta^s(t, t_0) - \Delta^s(t_0, t_0) = \int_{t_0}^t f(x_0(s - t_0)) \times g(x_0(s - t_0), s)\, ds$$

and, taking the limit $t \to +\infty$ and using the fact that $f(x_0(t)) \to f(p_0) = 0$ as $t \to \infty$, so that $\Delta^s(t, t_0) \to 0$, we obtain

$$(4.9) \qquad -\Delta^s(t_0, t_0) = \int_{t_0}^\infty (f \times g)(x_0(s - t_0), t)\, ds.$$

Note that we have used the validity of (4.3) on $[t_0, \infty)$ in this computation. Together with a similar computation for Δ^u, (4.9) yields

$$(4.10) \qquad \Delta^u(t_0, t_0) - \Delta^s(t_0, t_0) \overset{\text{def}}{=} M(t_0) = \int_{-\infty}^{\infty} (f \times g)(x_0(s - t_0), t) \, ds.$$

We have completed our sketch of the proof of

MELNIKOV'S THEOREM. *Under the hypotheses stated in* (4.1), *if $M(t_0)$ has simple zeros, then for $\varepsilon \neq 0$ sufficiently small the manifolds $W^s(p_\varepsilon)$, $W^u(p_\varepsilon)$ intersect transversely. If $M(t_0)$ is bounded away from zero then $W^s(p_\varepsilon) \cap W^u(p_\varepsilon) = 0$.*

We illustrate how easy the theorem is to apply by returning to our example (1.4). Here

$$(4.11) \qquad\qquad f = \begin{pmatrix} v \\ -\sin\theta \end{pmatrix}, \qquad \varepsilon g = \begin{pmatrix} 0 \\ \delta S(t) - \gamma v \end{pmatrix}.$$

The unperturbed homoclinic solution may be written

$$v(t - t_0) = \pm 2\,\text{sech}(t - t_0)$$

(we will not need the θ component), and to make explicit calculations we shall take

$$(4.12) \qquad\qquad \delta S(t) = \varepsilon \bar\delta \cos\omega t, \qquad \gamma = \varepsilon \bar\gamma,$$

so that the damping and applied torque are assumed to be small and of the same order. We then have $f \times g = \bar\delta v \cos\omega t - \gamma v^2$ and $M(t_0)$ may be written

$$(4.13) \quad M(t_0) = \pm 2\bar\delta \int_{-\infty}^{\infty} \text{sech}(\sigma) \cos\omega(\sigma + t_0) \, d\sigma - 4\gamma \int_{-\infty}^{\infty} \text{sech}^2(\sigma) \, d\sigma$$

after a change of variables $\sigma = s - t_0$. The second integral of (4.13) is elementary and the first can be evaluated by the method of residues to give

$$(4.14) \qquad\qquad M(t_0) = \pm 2\bar\delta\pi \, \text{sech}\,\frac{\pi\omega}{2} \cos\omega t_0 - 8\bar\gamma.$$

Clearly, $M(t_0)$ has simple zeros iff

$$(4.15) \qquad\qquad \bar\delta\pi > 4\bar\gamma \cosh\left(\frac{\pi\omega}{2}\right),$$

which is therefore an explicit criterion for the existence of transverse homoclinic orbits in the limit $\varepsilon \to 0$. Observe that this makes good physical sense. If dissipation $\gamma = \varepsilon\bar\gamma$ is large compared to force amplitude $\delta = \varepsilon\bar\delta$ then one does not expect recurrent behavior, since the pendulum will simply settle towards the stable position $(\theta, v) = (0, 0)$ as energy is absorbed and will asymptotically approach a (small) periodic solution about that equilibrium.

5. Conclusions. We now show that a remarkable physical conclusion follows from the analysis of the preceding sections. In Figure 7 we indicate how a modest generalization of the horseshoe arises in the Poincaré map of the perturbed pendulum. The "horizontal" strips H_R, H_L are carried by P^N into "vertical" strips V_R, V_L as indicated. Since the saddle points near (θ, v): $(\pm\pi, 0)$ are identified, these images intersect H_R, H_L much as in the canonical Smale example of Figure 5 (cf. Figure 4). As in §3, one obtains a homeomorphism between the shift on the two symbols R, L and some iterate P^N of the Poincaré map restricted to a suitable (Cantor) set $\Lambda^N = \bigcap_{n=-\infty}^{\infty} P^{nN}(H_R \cup H_L)$. Note that our construction guarantees that a point lying in H_R will be mapped around near the stable and unstable manifolds with $\dot\theta = v > 0$ while a point lying in H_L is mapped around with $\dot\theta < 0$. Thus, an 'R' in the symbol sequence corresponds to a passage of the pendulum bob past $\theta = 0$ with $\dot\theta > 0$ and an 'L' to a passage with $\dot\theta < 0$. Since we have a full shift ($P^N(H_L)$ and $P^N(H_R)$ both lie across $H_L \cup H_R$) we conclude that any "random" sequence of the symbols L, R corresponds to an orbit of the pendulum, rotating "chaotically" to the left and to the right.

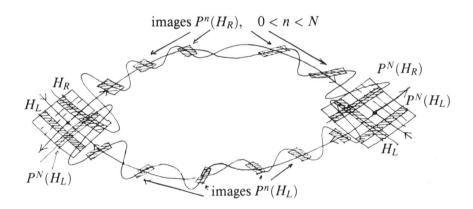

FIGURE 7. Poincaré map for the perturbed pendulum.

This conclusion is perhaps not too surprising, if we consider the effect of a small periodic perturbation on the unclamped, Hamiltonian pendulum swinging near its separatrix orbit $H(\theta, v) = 2$. Each time the pendulum reaches the top of its swing, near the inverted, unstable state, the oscillating torque supplies a small push either to the left or right depending on the phase (time). Thus the precise time at which the bob arrives near this position is crucial and this, in turn, is determined by the time at which it left the same position after the preceding swing. Here is the physical interpretation of sensitive dependence upon initial conditions.

At this point honesty compels us to point out that all is not rosy in the study of chaotic dynamics. The analysis sketched in this paper establishes

that a specific deterministic differential equation possesses chaotic orbits and
provides an estimate for the parameter range(s) in which they exist. This does
not necessarily imply that we have a *strange or chaotic attractor*. An *attractor*
for a flow or map is an *indecomposable, closed, invariant set* for the flow or
map, which attracts all orbits starting at points in some neighborhood. The
maximal such neighborhood is the *domain of attraction*, or *basin*. Jim Yorke's
lecture deals with this idea. In the pendulum example it is easy to see that
all orbits of P remain trapped in a band $\mathscr{B} = \{(\theta, v)||v| \leq \Gamma\}$ in the phase
space; one simply observes that, if we choose $\Gamma > \frac{1+S_{\max}}{\delta}$ ($S_{\max} = \max_t |S(t)|$),
then the second component of (1.4) admits the bounds

$$\dot{v} \leq |-\sin\theta| + \delta|S(t)| - \gamma|v|$$
$$\leq -\gamma|v| + 1 + \delta S_{\max}$$

for $v > 0$ and

$$\dot{v} \geq \gamma|v| - 1 - \delta S_{\max}$$

for $v < 0$. Thus the vector field points into the band $\mathscr{B}$ and hence it is
a forward invariant region for P ($P(\mathscr{B}) \subset \mathscr{B}$). The *attracting set* $\mathscr{A}$ is
the intersection of all forward images of $\mathscr{B}$ and, since $\det DP = e^{-\gamma T} < 1$
(equation (1.6)), P contracts areas by a constant factor and

$$\mathscr{A} = \bigcap_{n=0}^{\infty} P^n(\mathscr{B})$$

has zero area. $\mathscr{A}$ certainly contains the homoclinic points and their attendant
horseshoes displayed above, and any attractors are certainly contained in $\mathscr{A}$,
but $\mathscr{A}$ itself need not be indecomposable. To display parameter values for
which $\mathscr{A}$ *as a whole* and not just $\Lambda \subset \mathscr{A}$ has a dense orbit (or even a chain
recurrent dense orbit, cf. Guckenheimer and Holmes [1983]) appears very
difficult. In fact work of Newhouse [1980] on wild hyperbolic sets and the
presence of infinitely many stable periodic orbits at certain parameter values
for maps like P shows that there are a lot of values for which $\mathscr{A}$ *cannot* be
indecomposable. Thus a "typical" solution approaching $\mathscr{A}$ might eventually
settle down to stable periodic behavior, perhaps after a chaotic transient
played out near Λ. In spite of the suggestive nature of numerical simulations
(cf. Yorke's lecture), this issue still awaits clarification. I prefer to say that
P has a *strange attracting set*.

We conclude this article by remarking that the ideas we have outlined seem
to be of general relevance in the study of nonlinear differential equations arising in engineering and the sciences. It is now almost a commonplace that
"chaotic solutions" are observed in numerical simulation of diverse model
systems. Centers for nonlinear science are producing color graphics of fractals and strange attractors almost faster than one can look at them. However,
the tools introduced in this article, and especially the perturbative analytical

method of Melnikov, show that analysis can be brought to bear on these systems, and rigorous results obtained. Let us hope that their application brings some order into chaos.

References

A. A. Andronov, E. A. Vitt, and S. E. Khalkeii, [1966] *Theory of oscillators*, Pergamon Press New York.

V. I. Arnold [1964], *Instability of dynamical systems with several degrees of freedom*, Soviet Math. Dokl. **5** , 581–585.

V. I. Arnold [1973], *Ordinary differential equations*, M. I. T. Press.

V. I. Arnold [1982], *Geometrical methods in the theory of ordinary differential equations*, Springer-Verlag.

G. D. Birkhoff [1927], *Dynamical systems*, Amer. Math. Soc.

M. L. Cartwright and J. E. Littlewood [1945], *On nonlinear differential equations of the second order*, I: *the equation* $\ddot{y} + k(1 - y^2)\dot{y} + y = b\lambda k \cos(\lambda t + a), k$ *large*, J. London Math. Soc. **20**, 180–189.

R. L. Devaney [1986], *An introduction to chaotic dynamical systems*, Benjamin Cummings.

J. Guckenheimer and P. Holmes [1983], *Nonlinear oscillations, dynamical systems and bifurcation of vectorfields*, Springer-Verlag.

P. Holmes and J. E. Marsden [1981], *A partial differential equation with infinitely many periodic orbits: chaotic oscillations of a forced beam*, Arch. Rat. Mech. Anal. **76**, 135–166.

P. Holmes and J. E. Marsden [1982a], *Horseshoes in perturbations of Hamiltonians with two degrees of freedom*, Comm. Math. Phys. **82**, 523–544.

P. Holmes and J. E. Marsden [1982b], *Melnikov's method and Arnold diffusion for perturbations of integrable Hamiltonian systems*, J. Math. Phys. **23**, 669–675.

P. Holmes and J. E. Marsden [1983], *Horseshoes and Arnold diffusion for Hamiltonian systems on Lie groups*, Indiana Univ. Math. J. **32**, 273–310.

V. K. Melnikov [1983], *On the stability of the center for time periodic perturbations*, Trans. Moscow Math. Soc. **12**, 1–57.

J. Moser [1973], *Stable and random motions in dynamical systems*, Princeton University Press.

S. E. Newhouse [1980], Lectures on dynamical systems. In *Dynamical Systems*, CIME Lectures, Bressanone, Italy, June 1978, Birkhauser, pp. 1–114.

J. Palis and W. de Melo [1982], *Geometric theory of dynamical systems: An Introduction*, Springer-Verlag.

H. Poincaré [1890], *Sur le problème des trois corps et les équations de la dynamique*, mémoire Couronné du Prix de S. M. le Roi Oscar II, Paris, Acta Math. **13**, 1–271.

S. Smale [1963], Diffeomorphisms with many periodic points. In *Differential and Combinatorial Topology*, ed. S. S. Cairns, Princeton University Press, pp. 63–80.

S. Smale [1967], *Differential dynamical systems*, Bull. Amer. Math. Soc. **73**, 747–817.

S. Smale [1980], *The mathematics of time: essays on dynamical systems, economic processes and related topics*, Springer-Verlag.

S. Wiggins [1988], *Global bifurcations and chaos: analytic methods*, Springer-Verlag.

DEPARTMENTS OF THEORETICAL & APPLIED MECHANICS AND MATHEMATICS & CENTER FOR APPLIED MATHEMATICS, CORNELL UNIVERSITY, ITHACA, NEW YORK 14853

Proceedings of Symposia in Applied Mathematics
Volume 39, 1989

Fractal Basin Boundaries and Chaotic Attractors

KATHLEEN T. ALLIGOOD AND JAMES A. YORKE

1. Introduction. Trajectories that are exponentially unstable are nothing new to physical scientists. An attempt to balance a pin on its tip on a flat table is bound to fail. Almost any initial position near that unstable steady state will yield a trajectory that moves exponentially fast away from it: that is, the distance from the steady state will increase like $\exp(\lambda t)$ for some λ. This characteristic λ is called the Lyapunov exponent of the steady state. Of course the exponential growth is temporary. Once the pin falls over, the exponential growth has saturated and the distance no longer grows. The exponential growth rate characterizes only trajectories that are initially extremely close to the trajectory in question.

What is new to physical scientists, though, is the existence of exponentially unstable trajectories that are neither steady state nor periodic nor even asymptotic to steady state or periodic trajectories. We will say a trajectory is *a chaotic trajectory* if it is exponentially unstable, i.e., has a Lyapunov exponent λ that is positive, and if it is neither periodic nor asymptotic to a periodic trajectory. Such trajectories are observed to oscillate irregularly for all time without settling down. The article by Phillip Holmes in this volume describes horseshoe maps. Such maps contain uncountably many initial points which yield chaotic trajectories. The article by Linda Keen describes Julia sets which usually contain uncountably many chaotic trajectories.

Dynamical systems can have many coexisting attractors. In order to predict the behavior of such a dynamical system, it is important to recognize to which of these attractors a given trajectory will converge. The set of initial conditions whose orbits (i.e., trajectories) are asymptotic to a particular attractor is called the *basin of attraction* of that attractor. The boundaries between respective basins of attraction can exhibit very complicated behavior. In particular, they often contain chaotic trajectories. We begin with a one-dimensional example, in which the boundary between two basins is a Cantor set.

1980 *Mathematics Subject Classification* (1985 *Revision*). Primary 58Fxx.

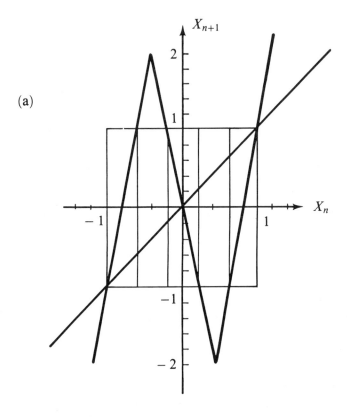

(a)

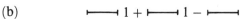

(b)

(c)

FIGURE 1. (a) The map $x_{n+1} = F(x_n)$. (b) The interval
1+ (resp., 1−) maps in one iterate to $x > 1$ (resp. $x <$
-1). (c) The intervals 2+ (resp., 2−) map in two iterates
to $x > 1$ (resp., $x < -1$).

The specific map F which we investigate is piecewise linear and is illustrated in Figure 1a. This map has only two attractors, namely, $x = +\infty$ and
$x = -\infty$. Let $x_{n+1} = F(x_n)$. Then, for any point $x_n > 1$, the map may be
expressed

$$(x_{n+1} - 1) = 5(x_n - 1).$$

Any initial condition in $x > 1$ generates an orbit which tends to $+\infty$, and thus $x > 1$ is part of the basin for the $x = +\infty$ attractor. By symmetry, $x < -1$ is part of the basin of the $x = -\infty$ attractor. From Figure 1a we also see that the points $0.2 < x < 0.6$ (resp., $-0.6 < x < -0.2$) map in one iterate into $x < -1$ (resp., $x > +1$). Hence, $0.2 < x < 0.6$ is in the $-\infty$ basin, and $0.6 < x < 0.2$ is in the $+\infty$ basin. This is illustrated in Figure 1b [the symbol 1+ (resp., 1−) signifies that the designated interval maps to $x > +1$ (resp., $x < -1$) in one iterate of the map]. Continuing the construction, one finds three open intervals which map to the 1+ interval in one iterate and hence to $x > 1$ in two iterates. (These intervals are labeled 2+ in Figure 1c.) Three more open intervals (labeled 2−) map to $x < -1$ in two iterates. The 2+ (resp., 2−) intervals are in the basin of $+\infty$ (resp., $-\infty$). Thus the basin boundary must lie in $[-1, +1]$ and does not contain any of the eight intervals labeled $1+, 1-, 2+$, or $2-$. As one continues taking out open sets, one recognizes the boundary between the two basins as a standard Cantor set. As we will see, the Cantor set structure of this simple example turns out to be a recurring theme in the description of basin boundaries. (For further discussion of this map, see [10].)

In the following sections we concentrate on invertible maps of the real plane $\mathbf{R}^2$. It is possible for the boundary between two basins to be very simple. Consider the smooth invertible map of the plane defined by $F(r, \theta) = (r^2, \theta - \sin\theta)$, where $r \geq 0$ and $0 \leq \theta < 2\pi$ are polar coordinates. The attractors are the origin and infinity, and the boundary between them is the unit circle. See Figure 2. Every initial condition inside the circle tends toward the origin upon iteration, and every point outside the circle tends toward infinity. The dynamics on the dividing circle is also rather tame: there is a fixed point at $(r, \theta) = (1, 0)$ to which all points on the circle tend, except for the fixed point $(r, \theta) = (1, \pi)$. The basin boundary itself is unstable, in that points near it are repelled, except for points precisely on the boundary.

It turns out that the boundary between two basins can be far more complicated than a simple curve and may contain chaotic trajectories. The following example illustrates some of the possibilities. Consider a square that is mapped to an S-shaped configuration, mapping across itself in three strips. (See Figure 3.) It also has two attracting points outside the square, and we might assume legitimately that all points in the square that are mapped to the left of the square eventually go to the attractor on the left and all points in this square that are mapped to the right of the square will eventually go to the attractor on the right. Now consider a curve γ that runs from the left of the square to the right side of the square more or less monotonically. Since γ is in the square, its image under the map will lie in the S shape. Notice that the ends of γ and two intermediate pieces of γ map outside S, so we can determine to which attractor those points will eventually go. However there are three segments of γ that map into S. The image of each of these pieces maps across S just as γ did. We label the segments of γ that stay inside by $\gamma 1$,

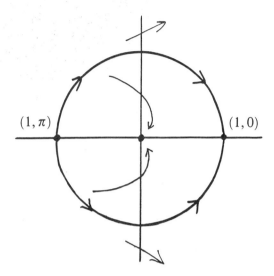

FIGURE 2. The point $(0,0)$ is an attractor for the map $F(r,\theta) = (r^2, \theta - \sin\theta)$. Its basin of attraction is the interior of the unit disk. The dynamics on the basin boundary, the unit circle, are shown. Except for the fixed point $(1,\pi)$, the orbits of all points on the basin boundary are asymptotic to the fixed point $(1,0)$.

$\gamma 2$, and $\gamma 3$. Since the image $F(\gamma 1)$ stretches across the square, there will be three segments of the $\gamma 1$ image which in turn stay inside the square for one iterate. It follows that there will be three segments on $\gamma 1$ that remain inside the square for two iterates. The same is true of $\gamma 2$ and $\gamma 3$. This approach implies that the subset of γ that remains inside the square for n iterates consists of 3^n segments. Each of these segments has three subsegments which will remain inside the square for a total of $n + 1$ iterates. If we have set up the map in a reasonable manner, the size of the segments at the nth stage will shrink geometrically to zero as n tends to ∞. Thus we have a standard Cantor set construction; that is, there is a Cantor set of points on γ whose trajectories will remain inside for all future time.

When we examine a segment like $\gamma 1$ and observe that it has three subsegments which remain inside the square, we also see there are two segments, γ_L and γ_R, that lie between these three segments. These two segments will go to the two different attractors. Each point of the Cantor set then has segments of γ nearby which go to the left attractor and also segments nearby which go to the right attractor. Therefore such points are basin boundary points.

Two trajectories which start out close together on γ will diverge exponentially fast, more than tripling the distance between them on each iterate. Of

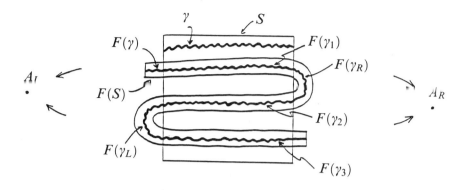

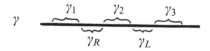

FIGURE 3. A square S is mapped to an S-shaped configuration. There are two attracting fixed points A_L and
A_R outside the square. All points in the square that map
to the left (resp., right) of the square eventually go to A_L
(resp., A_R). As described in the text, the boundary between the two basins of attraction intersects the square
in a Cantor set of nearly vertical lines.

course, this tripling will not continue forever since they will never become
further apart than the distance between two attractors.

We have described what happens on a line of initial conditions γ. Since
the square can be viewed as a union of horizontal parallel lines, we can repeat
the same construction for each of these lines. For each basin boundary point
p on γ there will be a nearly vertical curve of basin boundary points through
p. Thus the basin boundary in this square is a Cantor set of nearly vertical
lines. Each of these vertical lines stretches from the top of the square to the
bottom of the square. Let V be such a vertical line segment in S. Its image
$F(V)$ will be inside $F(S)$, and so will be a short vertical curve. Since this
short vertical curve is on the boundary and since basin boundary points map
to basin boundary points, it must be on one of the vertical curves of the basin
boundary which stretches from top to bottom.

Now if we ask which points of the vertical curve V stay in the square
as we iterate backwards in time, we find the argument is somewhat similar

to the original Cantor set construction. Since V cuts across $F(S)$ in three intervals which we call V_1, V_2, and V_3, the points in V whose inverse will also be in S consists of $V_1 \cup V_2 \cup V_3$. For example, $F^{-1}(V_1)$ is a nearly vertical strip stretching from the top to the bottom of the square. If we consider further the second inverse iterate, we find V_1 itself contains three small segments of points that remain inside as for two consecutive iterates. Continuing the argument, we find that these contain a Cantor set of points remaining inside S for all backwards iterates of F. Therefore the set of points which remain inside for all backwards iterates will consist of a Cantor set of horizontal segments. The set of points that remain inside as for all forward and backward iterates of F then is the intersection of a Cantor set of horizontal lines with a Cantor set of vertical lines. This Cantor set is the invariant set of F in S. As follows from the article by Holmes, points that are on periodic orbits are dense in the invariant set. They are countable in number, however, while the set itself is uncountable.

The example of Figure 3, although more complicated than the example of Figure 2, is still almost pathologically well behaved. At each point of the invariant set there is a contracting direction which is more or less vertical and there is an expanding direction which is more or less horizontal. For this reason we can say the invariant set of Figure 3 is uniformly hyperbolic.

Computer studies show us that basin boundaries in fact usually lack this uniformly hyperbolic structure and are significantly more complicated. The study of chaotic dynamics often involves numerical studies of actual situations coupled with theoretical studies of unrealistically nice systems that are uniformly hyperbolic. When we understand the simple cases such as the example above, we hope to have gained considerable understanding of more complicated situations. When we appeal to the theories of what these boundary sets might look like, and construct paper and pencil examples that we can actually analyze, the results are always quite mild compared with what the computer actually tells us the real examples are like. Thus we are particularly pleased to be able to report in this paper that the structure of basin boundaries is in some ways very regular and can be shown rigorously to have a regular structure.

A basin with a smooth boundary is depicted in Figure 4a, and one with a fractal boundary is shown in Figure 4b. The underlying dynamical system (map of the plane) is given by the Ikeda map:

$$F(x, y) = (\gamma + \beta(x \cos \tau - y \sin \tau), \beta(x \sin \tau + y \cos \tau))$$

where $\tau = \mu - \alpha/(1 + x^2 + y^2)$. This map was proposed in [13] as a model, under some simplifying assumptions, of the type of cell that may be used in a laser computer. The map is invertible with Jacobian determinant β^2. For $|\beta| < 1$, the map is area-contracting. For area-contracting maps, basins must have infinite area. This follows from the fact that they are invariant under the map (and have positive area). In certain ranges of the parameters, there are two attracting fixed points, corresponding to two stable light frequencies

(a)

(b)

FIGURE 4. The basins of two fixed point attractors of
the Ikeda map are shown in black and white. The x and
y values are in the rectangle $[-2.3, 1.3] \times [-2.8, 0.8]$.
In (a), at parameter $\gamma = .92$, the boundary is smooth
(locally connected) and is composed of a fixed point
saddle p and its stable manifold. In (b), at $\gamma = 1.0$,
the basin boundary is fractal. At this parameter value,
the only accessible points are the four periodic points
(labelled 1, 2, 3, and 4) of a period four orbit and their
stable manifolds.

in the cell. Parameters β, μ, and α are fixed at .9, .4, and 4.0, respectively, within the range of bistability.

In Figure 4a, the basins of attraction of the two attracting fixed points are shown for parameter $\gamma = .92$. One attractor A_1 (not shown) is in the black region, and the forward orbits of almost all points in the black region converge to it. The other attractor A_2 is in the white region and the forward orbits of almost all orbits in the white region converge to it. No points in the white (resp., black) region are in the basin of A_1 (resp., A_2). The boundary between the basins of A_1 and A_2 is observed numerically to consist of a saddle fixed point p and its stable manifold $W^s(p)$. (The *stable manifold $W^s(p)$* of a fixed point p is the set of points (x, y) such that $F^n(x, y) \to p$, as $n \to \infty$. More generally, the stable manifold $W^s(p_k)$ of a periodic point p_k is the set of points (x, y) such that $F^{nk}(x, y) \to p_k$, as $n \to \infty$. Analogously, the *unstable manifold $W^u(p_k)$* of p_k is the set of points (x, y) such that $F^{-nk}(x, y) \to p_k$, as $n \to \infty$. For a saddle in the plane, such sets are smooth curves.)

In Figure 4b, the parameter γ is set at 1.0, and the boundary is fractal. Its Hausdorff dimension is a noninteger value between one and two. Roughly speaking, the boundary is locally the cross product of a Cantor set and a line segment. It is not locally connected. In addition, buried within the fractal layers of the boundary are saddle periodic orbits of arbitrarily high periods. In both cases (a) and (b) the basins have infinite area.

Even though the dynamics on the boundary appear to be very complicated, it has been observed (see, for example, [10]) that some points on the boundary exhibit regular behavior. We say that a point p on the boundary of an open set W is *accessible* from W if there is a path beginning in W such that p is the first point not in W which the path hits. For the boundary shown in Figure 4b, most points are not accessible. For this map (Figure 4b), there are four points that are saddles of period four (i.e., one period-four orbit) which are accessible from the white region, and all other points which are accessible from the white region are on the stable manifolds of these periodic points.

In §2, we investigate the dynamics of the accessible points on basin boundaries. The ideas presented are strongly motivated by numerical studies that repeatedly conclude there are accessible periodic saddles in the boundary. In fact, we know of no case of an area-contracting diffeomorphism having a basin boundary without accessible periodic orbits. In §3, we describe *basin boundary metamorphoses*, that is, sudden jumps of the boundary which occur as a parameter as the dynamical system is varied. In §4, we apply the theory to a class of chaotic attractors, viewed as basin boundaries for the inverse of the map.

2. The dynamics of accessible orbits. Let W be a connected, simply connected open set either in the plane or in the sphere S^2. Such a set must be topologically an open disk. Our main examples of such sets will be basins of attraction. In particular, the basin of attraction of an attracting fixed point must be such a set. On the other hand, the boundary B of such a region does not have to be topologically a circle, and examples abound in which the boundary of a basin of attraction is a fractal set. The characterization of a set W as a topological open disk occurs in the study of the Riemann Mapping Theorem which says that for any such set W there is always a one-to-one analytic map h of an open disk D onto W. This characterization of a basin as being an open disk tells us nothing about the boundary of a basin, and it is our objective to describe the dynamics on the points in B that are accessible from W.

In the following we say that p is *accessible* only if it is a point of B that is accessible from W. We assume throughout that B contains more than one point.

Carathéodory [5] investigated the behavior of the map h in the Riemann mapping theorem to see when h could be defined at boundary points of the disk. If Γ is a (continuous) path in W which limits on the accessible point p, then $h^{-1}(\Gamma)$ is a (continuous) path in D limiting on exactly one point r in S^1. We call such points as r *trivial circle points*; we call all other points on the circle *nontrivial circle points*. Carathéodory's approach was to construct a compactification of W which is topologically identical to $\overline{D}$, the closed disk. (This is not the standard compactification; points in this compactification which correspond to points in the boundary S^1 of $\overline{D}$ are called "prime ends". A general reference for the theory of prime ends is [8, Chapter 9].)

We define a map h_c on points in D and on trivial circle points by $h_c(x) = h(x)$ for x in D, and $h_c(r) = p$ where p is an accessible point and r is an associated trivial circle point, as defined above. It is clear from the construction that each accessible point is the image of at least one trivial circle point. (The map h_c is not necessarily one-to-one on trivial circle points.)

We mention two properties of accessible points and the map h_c:

PROPERTY 1 (DENSITY). The set of accessible points is dense in B; the set of trivial circle points is dense in S^1.

PROPERTY 2 (EXISTENCE OF AN INDUCED MAP). For any homeomorphism F of the closure of W into itself such that $F(W) = W$, there is a map, denoted f and called the *induced map*, from $\overline{D}$ to itself such that $h_c(f(x)) = F(h_c(x))$ when x is in D or x is a trivial circle point.

The induced map f of Property 2 is a homeomorphism and is completely determined on S^1 by its action on the trivial circle points, since by Property 1 such points are dense in S^1. If p is an accessible point and Γ is a path in W ending at p, then $F(\Gamma)$ is a path in W ending at $F(p)$. Hence, accessible points map to accessible points. It follows that f maps trivial circle points to trivial circle points.

These properties allow us to study the dynamical system on the closed disk, maintaining the dynamics on the accessible points. Since in general B will include much more than the accessible points, much of B is lost in this representation. However, for us, the simplification is advantageous since we wish to describe the dynamics on the accessible points.

We have important examples in which W is not a basin even though a dense set of points in W have trajectories tending to an attractor. The following definition allows the inclusion of such examples. Let V_R be the set of points in $\mathbf{R}^2$ with norm greater than R. We say that B is *unstable in W* if there exist a neighborhood B_ε of B and a number $R > 0$ such that the set of points in $V = B_\varepsilon \cup V_R$ whose orbits eventually leave V is dense in $V \cap W$. (I.e., there is a dense set Q in $V \cap W$ such that $x \in Q$ implies that $F^n(x)$ is in $W \setminus V$ for some $n > 0$.) This definition is easily seen to be satisfied when W is a basin of attraction. It is also satisfied in the very different case where there is a dense orbit in W.

Certain types of periodic orbits in S^1 merit particular attention. Let $p \in S^1$ be a periodic point of period k. We say p is *weakly repelling* (in S^1) if there is no x in S^1 such that $\lim_{n \to \infty} f^{nk}(x) = p$.

The following key theorem is proved in [3]:

THEOREM 2.1 (REPELLING LEMMA). *Let F be a homeomorphism of W. Assume that B is invariant under F and that it is unstable in W. Assume further that for each n the periodic points of F of period n are isolated in B. Then each nontrivial circle point that is periodic under f is weakly repelling for f restricted to S^1.*

The study of homeomorphisms of the circle is classical. Poincaré showed that associated with each orientation-preserving homeomorphism γ of the circle is a "rotation" number, an asymptotic measure of the rotation of points on the circle under iteration by γ. Here we mention briefly some facts about these maps which are needed in the arguments that follow. A reference for this material is [9].

In order to define the rotation number, it is convenient first to consider a "lift" of γ. A map G of $\mathbf{R}$ is called a *lift* of γ if $\pi \circ G = \gamma \circ \pi$, where π is the covering map from $\mathbf{R}$ to S^1; i.e., $\pi(x) = \exp(2\pi i x)$. Let

$$p_G(x) = \lim_{n \to \infty} G^n(x)/n, \quad \text{for } x \text{ in } S^1.$$

Fact C1. The value $p_G(x)$ is independent of both x and the particular lift G of γ.

We define the *rotation number* $r(\gamma)$ of γ to be the fractional part of $p_G(x)$ for any point x on S^1 and any lift G of γ. That is, $r(\gamma)$ is the unique number r in $[0, 1)$ such that $p_G(x) - r$ is an integer. By Fact C1, $r(\gamma)$ is well defined.

Fact C2. A map γ of the circle has points of *minimum* period q if and only if $r(\gamma)$ is an irreducible fraction of the form p/q, for some positive integer p. The map γ has fixed points if and only if $r(\gamma) = 0$.

Thus, if γ has periodic points, they must all have the same period.

Fact C3. If γ has a periodic point of period n, then every point on the circle is either a fixed point of γ^n or is asymptotic to a fixed point under iterates of γ^n.

We define the *rotation number* $\rho(W, F)$ of an orientation-preserving homeomorphism F on the accessible points of W to be the rotation number of the induced map f on S^1. If W is a connected, simply-connected open set in $\mathbf{R}^2$ and if the closure of W is invariant under F, then W has a rotation number. In particular, if p is an isolated, attracting fixed point in $\mathbf{R}^2$ and if its basin W is not all of $\mathbf{R}^2$, then W has a rotation number (see [3]). In the example of Figure 2, the basin W of the attractor $(0,0)$ is the unit disk. The rotation number of F on the set of accessible boundary points (which is the entire unit circle) is 0. For the examples in Figure 4a and 4b, the rotation numbers on the points accessible from the white basin are 0 and $1/4$, respectively.

G. D. Birkhoff recognized that the set of accessible points is dense in the boundary of an invariant region and that their dynamics can be characterized by their rotation number. He used this idea in [4] to construct a map of the annulus into itself with an unusual invariant set J. On one hand, J resembles a closed Jordan curve in that each of its points is on the boundary of both an interior region S_{int} (containing one boundary circle of the annulus) and an exterior region S_{ext} (containing the other boundary circle). On the other hand, J is "remarkable" in the sense that it contains a dense set of points accessible from S_{int} with one rotation number and a dense set accessible from S_{ext} with a different rotation number. To compare this situation with our hypotheses, notice that such a map has an inverse for which J is unstable (in S_{int} and in S_{ext}) and J is the boundary between the points which go outward and those which go inward (under the inverse).

Cartwright and Littlewood further developed these ideas in [6], where they study questions of existence and stability of fixed points and periodic points for maps of the plane—questions motivated by their work in differential equations (see [7]). The idea of associating a rotation number to the boundary of a simply-connected region was used by Cartwright and Littlewood in [6]. More recently, J. Mather has given purely topological proofs of some of the topological results of Carathéodory in [16].

The following argument explains the significance of the Repelling Lemma. Assume that the rotation number of f on S^1 is rational (say the reduced fraction p/q). Then S^1 will have at least one fixed point under f^q (i.e., a periodic point of period q). If a trivial circle point x is not fixed under f^q, then its orbit converges to a fixed point r under iterates of f^q. By the Repelling Lemma, r is necessarily a trivial circle point. Corresponding to r is an accessible point p on B. By Property 2, p is fixed under F^q. Thus we have the following result [3]:

THEOREM 2.2. *Let F be an orientation-preserving homeomorphism of the closure of W onto itself. Assume that for each n the periodic orbits of F of period n are isolated and that B is invariant under F and unstable in W. Assume further that the rotation number $\rho(B, F)$ is p/q (resp., 0). Then there is an accessible fixed point of F^q (resp., F) on B.*

Note. In [3] we give a complete characterization of the accessible boundary points when the rotation number is rational. There, under some additional hypotheses, we prove that all accessible points are on the stable manifolds of accessible periodic orbits. The additional hypotheses are that periodic points on the boundary are hyperbolic and that ∞ is repelling in the basin.

3. Basin boundary metamorphoses.

For an orientation-preserving homeomorphism of the circle that depends on a scalar parameter, the rotation number varies continuously with the parameter. For the basin boundary of a map of the plane, such as described in the previous sections, the rotation number of the accessible points does not necessarily vary continuously with changes in a parameter. As a parameter is varied, a basin boundary can jump suddenly, and, as it does, change from being smooth to fractal. Such changes are called *basin boundary metamorphoses*. Figure 4 shows part of a basin boundary before (4a) and after (4b) a metamorphosis. In Figure 4a, the basins of attraction of two attracting fixed points are shown for parameter $\gamma = .92$ (see §1). The basin of the attractor A_1 is shown in black. In Figure 4b, the parameter γ is increased to 1.0, and the basin of A_1 now contains points which previously (at $\gamma = .92$) were well within the white region. This new set of black points has not moved in gradually from the boundary of the white region. Rather, beyond a certain critical value $\gamma = \gamma_* \approx .93$, black points suddenly begin appearing deep within the interior of the white region. This is a discontinuous change in the basin of A_1. In addition, for $\gamma > \gamma_*$ the boundary is fractal.

As described in §1, the boundary between the two basins shown in Figure 4a is observed numerically to consist of a saddle fixed point p and its stable manifold $W^s(p)$. One branch of the unstable manifold $W^u(p)$ at $\gamma = .92$ extends into the white region. At the critical value $\gamma = \gamma_*$, after which the basin boundary jumps into the white region, $W^s(p)$ and $W^u(p)$ are tangent and then cross for $\gamma > \gamma_*$. S. Hammel and C. Jones [12] were the first to prove a theorem relating the tangency of $W^s(p)$ and $W^u(p)$ (called a *homoclinic tangency*) to boundary metamorphoses. In [10] and [2], these metamorphoses are explained in terms of saddle periodic orbits which are found near the points of tangency and their stable and unstable manifolds.

Let q be a point at which $W^s(p)$ and $W^u(p)$ are tangent. Under certain nondegeneracy assumptions (see, for example, [11]), there is a number $N > 0$ and a sequence $\{p_n\}_{n>N}$ of periodic saddles such that the period of p_n is n and $\lim_{n\to\infty} p_n = q$. Each p_n is in the interior of the white region for $\gamma \leq \gamma_*$, a positive distance from the boundary $W^s(p)$.

The following theorem was originally stated in [10] and later proved (with nondegeneracy assumptions) in [2]. The saddle orbit T as mentioned in the theorem corresponds to one of the sequence $\{p_n\}$ of saddle periodic orbits described in the previous paragraph.

THEOREM 3.1. *Consider an invertible map F of the plane depending on a parameter γ with a saddle fixed point or periodic orbit p. Assume that the absolute value of the Jacobian determinant of F (or of F^n, in the case of a periodic orbit of period n) is less than one at every point of the plane. Assume further that F has a transition value γ_*, as γ increases, where the stable and unstable manifolds of p have a nondegenerate tangency and then cross for the first time. Then there will be a periodic saddle T that is in the closure of the stable manifold of p for all γ slightly greater than γ_*, but is not in it at γ_*. This saddle T is a positive distance from the stable manifold of p for $\gamma = \gamma_*$.*

For the example described above and shown in Figure 4, the boundary jumps in to a period-four saddle at $\gamma = \gamma_*$. Thus the rotation number jumps from 0 to 1/4 at this parameter value. The evolution of rotation numbers of accessible points as a prototypical map undergoes successive metamorphoses is described in [1].

4. Rotation numbers for chaotic attractors. Here we look at a class $\mathscr{A}$ of nonperiodic attractors: an attractor Θ is in $\mathscr{A}$ if Θ is compact, connected, invariant under F, contains more than one point, and is not all fixed points. Typically, such sets will contain chaotic trajectories. In order to apply Theorem 2.2, we show how to assign a rotation number to an attractor in the class $\mathscr{A}$. This approach is reminiscent of Birkhoff [4] and also of Cartwright and Littlewood [7] and Levinson [15] who studied attractors in forced van der Pol type equations.

In looking at the Poincaré map of such equations, Cartwright and Littlewood showed that there are invariant annuli which have unequal rotation numbers on the boundary circles and which possess strange attracting sets. Each such attractor is the boundary of the inside contracting and outside contracting parts of the annulus. The existence of different rotation numbers inherited from the boundary circles was evidence to them of a continuum attractor which was not homeomorphic to S^1. Levinson gave a careful analysis of the attracting invariant set of a piecewise-linear version of this map in [15]. His work set the stage for the discovery of the horseshoe map by Smale. See also Levi's analysis of forced van der Pol type equations in [14].

In the following lemma, we assume that F is area contracting. Let $\mathscr{Z} = \mathbf{R}^2 \cup \{\infty\}$ be the one-point compactification of $\mathbf{R}^2$.

LEMMA 4.1. *If Θ is in $\mathscr{A}$, then $\mathscr{Z} - \Theta$ is connected and simply-connected in $\mathscr{Z}$.*

PROOF. Since Θ is connected, each component of $\mathscr{Z} - \Theta$ is simply connected in $\mathscr{Z}$. Since Θ is compact, only one component D_∞ of $\mathbf{R}^2 - \Theta$ has infinite area (in $\mathbf{R}^2$) and, given any bound η, there are only finitely many other components with area larger than η. Let D_M be a component of $\mathbf{R}^2 - \Theta$ with maximum finite area in $\mathbf{R}^2$. Since F^{-1} is area-expanding and components of $\mathbf{R}^2 - \Theta$ map onto other components of $\mathbf{R}^2 - \Theta$, F^{-1} maps D_M onto D_∞. But F^{-1} also maps D_∞ onto D_∞, contradicting the fact that F^{-1} is a homeomorphism. Thus $\mathscr{Z} - \Theta$ is connected and simply-connected in $\mathscr{Z}$. $\quad\square$

Now we can apply Theorem 2.2 to Θ, which is the boundary of the open, connected, simply-connected region $\mathscr{Z} - \Theta$. By looking at F^{-1} instead of F, it can be shown that Θ is unstable in $\mathscr{Z} - \Theta$, as follows. Let Θ_ε be an ε-neighborhood of Θ, and let D be an open set in $\Theta_\varepsilon \cap (\mathscr{Z} - \Theta)$. Since F^{-1} is *area-expanding*, the area enclosed by the boundary of D becomes unbounded under iteration by F^{-1}. Thus there are points in D whose orbits must eventually leave Θ_ε, and Θ is unstable in $\mathscr{Z} - \Theta$ under F^{-1}. Theorem 2.2 provides the following result:

PROPOSITION 4.2. *Let F be an area-contracting homeomorphism of the plane, and let Θ be in the class $\mathscr{A}$ of attractors. Assume that, for each n, the periodic points of F of period n are isolated. If the rotation number $\rho(\mathscr{Z} - \Theta, F)$ is the reduced fraction p/q, then there is an accessible fixed point of F^q on Θ.*

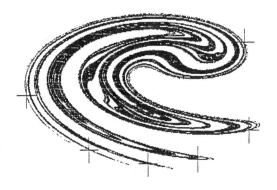

FIGURE 5. A chaotic attractor of the Ikeda map $F(x,y) = (0.97+0.9(x \cos \tau - y \sin \tau), 0.9(x \sin \tau + y \cos \tau))$, where $\tau = 0.4 - 6.0/(1.0 + x^2 + y^2)$, is shown. There is an accessible period 6 orbit on the attractor.

Figure 5 shows an attractor for the Ikeda map (see §1) with an accessible period 6 orbit. For a typical area-contracting diffeomorphism depending on a parameter λ, we conjecture that the rotation number $\rho(\lambda)$ will vary continuously, except possibly at a discrete set of values of λ, and that $\rho(\lambda)$ will be irrational for a nonempty set of λ of measure 0.

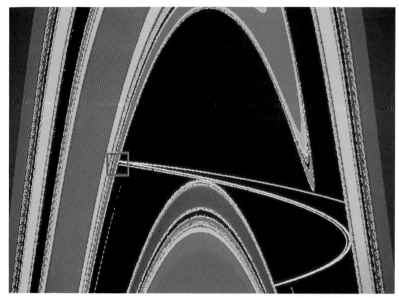

COLOR PLATE 1a

COLOR PLATE 1b

Successive computer magnifications of a fractal basin boundary for the Hénon map

$$F(x, y) = (A - x^2 + By, x),$$

with $A = 2.124$ and $B = -0.3$. The first picture has (x, y) values in the rectangle $[-2.2, 2.25] \times [-1.25, 5]$. There is a one-piece chaotic attractor shown in yellow. Points are colored according to the escape time of the trajectory beginning at that point. The escape time is defined to be the number of iterates necessary for the trajectory to leave a large square containing the original region. There is an accessible period three saddle on the basin boundary. The Hénon map pictures (Color Plates 1 and 2) were made using "Dynamics, a Program for IBM-PC Clones," by J. Yorke. All of the pictures (Color Plates 1–4) were made by photographing a computer screen.

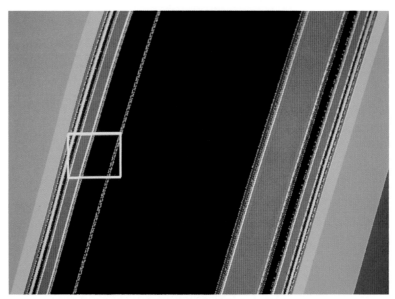

COLOR PLATE 1c

COLOR PLATE 1d

COLOR PLATE 2

A chaotic attractor (in white) of the Hénon map at A = 1.4 and B = 0.3. There is an accessible fixed point on the attractor and an accessible fixed point on the boundary of its basin of attraction. Each trajectory that begins at a point colored blue goes to infinity in norm; trajectories of points colored black and red go to the attractor. The red points are on the stable manifold of the accessible fixed point on the attractor.

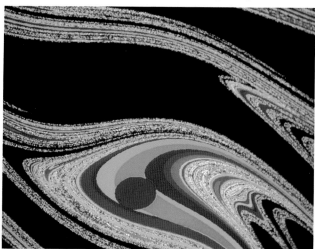

COLOR PLATE 3

Basins of attraction of the forced, damped pendulum equation

$$\ddot{\theta} + k\dot{\theta} + \sin \theta = \rho \cos t$$

with damping constant k = 0.2 and ρ = 2. Each point in the picture represents the initial position of a trajectory. There are two attracting periodic orbits. The points whose trajectories converge to the first of the attractors are colored according to their convergence time. The convergence time is the number of iterates necessary for a trajectory to enter the blue disk neighborhood of the attractor. All other points, including those whose trajectories converge to the second attractor, are colored black. The x and y coordinates are the initial angle and initial velocity; therefore, the left and right sides (θ = −π and θ = π) are identified. The pendulum pictures (Color Plates 3 and 4) were made by Frank Varosi and the University of Maryland.

COLOR PLATE 4a

COLOR PLATE 4b

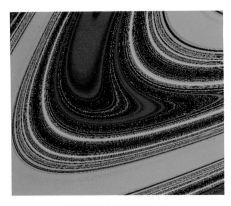

COLOR PLATE 4c

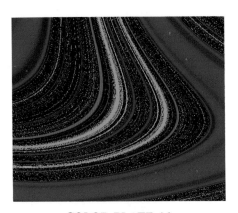

COLOR PLATE 4d

Successive computer magnifications of basins of attraction of the forced, damped pendulum with $k = 0.1$ and $\rho = 1.75$. There are four attracting periodic orbits. The initial conditions whose orbits converge to each of the four attractors are colored red, blue, yellow, and green, respectively. The darker the shade, the longer the convergence time.

References

1. K. Alligood and T. Sauer, *Rotation numbers of periodic orbits in the Hénon map*, Comm. Math. Phys. **120** (1988), 105–119.

2. K. Alligood, L. Tedeschini-Lalli, and J. Yorke, *Metamorphoses: sudden jumps in basin boundaries*, preprint.

3. K. Alligood and J. Yorke, *Accessible saddles on fractal basin boundaries*, preprint.

4. G. D. Birkhoff, *Sur quelques courbes fermées remarquables*, Bull. Soc. Math. France **60** (1932), 1–26.

5. C. Carathéodory, *Über die Begrenzung einfach zusammenhängender Gebiete*, Math. Ann. **73** (1913), 323–370.

6. M. L. Cartwright and J. E. Littlewood, *Some fixed point theorems*, Ann. of Math. (2) **54** (1951), 1–37.

7. ____, *On non-linear differential equations of the second order*: I. *The equation* $y'' - k(1 - y^2)y' + y = b\lambda k \cos(\lambda t + \alpha)$, *k large*, J. London Math. Soc. **20** (1945), 180–189.

8. E. F. Collingwood and A. J. Lohwater, *Theory of cluster sets*, Cambridge Tracts in Mathematics and Mathematical Physics, No. 56, Cambridge Univ. Press, 1966.

9. R. L. Devaney, *An introduction to chaotic dynamical systems*, Benjamin/Cummings, Menlo Park, 1986.

10. C. Grebogi, E. Ott, and J. Yorke, *Basin boundary metamorphoses: changes in accessible boundary orbits*, Physica **24D** (1987), 243–262.

11. N. Gavrilov and L. Silnikov, *On the three dimensional dynamical systems close to a system with a structurally unstable homoclinic curve*. I, Math. USSR Sbornik **17** (1972), 467–485; II, Math USSR Sbornik **19** (1973), 139–156.

12. S. Hammel and C. Jones, *Jumping stable manifolds for dissipative maps of the plane*, preprint.

13. S. Hammel, C. Jones, and J. Moloney, *Global dynamical behavior of the optical field in a ring cavity*, J. Opt. Soc. Amer. B **2** (1985), 552–564.

14. M. Levi, *Qualitative analysis of the periodically forced relaxation oscillations*, Mem. Amer. Math. Soc. No. 214 (1981).

15. N. Levinson, *A second order differential equation with singular solutions*, Ann. of Math. (2) **50** (1947), 127–153.

16. J. Mather, *Topological proofs of some purely topological consequences of Caratheódory's theory of prime ends*, Th. M. Rassias, G. M. Rassias, eds., Selected Studies, North-Holland, 1982, pp. 225–255.

DEPARTMENT OF MATHEMATICAL SCIENCES, GEORGE MASON UNIVERSITY, FAIRFAX, VIRGINIA 22030

DEPARTMENT OF MATHEMATICS AND INSTITUTE FOR PHYSICAL SCIENCE AND TECHNOLOGY, UNIVERSITY OF MARYLAND, COLLEGE PARK, MARYLAND 20742

Proceedings of Symposia in Applied Mathematics
Volume **39**, 1989

Julia Sets

LINDA KEEN

In the first lecture of this course, Devaney discussed one dimensional real dynamical systems. He analyzed the systems generated by $x^2 + c$ for various values of the real parameter c. In the next lectures, Holmes and Yorke discussed how much more complicated two dimensional real dynamical systems can be. Here, we study one dimensional complex analytic systems; the pictures are two dimensional and more interesting than in the real one dimensional case but because the maps are complex analytic, the theory is much closer to the real one dimensional case than to the real two dimensional case. All of our systems exhibit what Devaney defines as " chaotic behavior."

Devaney began with quadratic maps on the line. The natural complexification is to quadratic maps of the complex plane. There are, however, advantages to studying dynamical systems on compact spaces, and we therefore think of the quadratic map as a map of the Riemann sphere to itself which fixes the point at infinity. As such, it is an example of a rational map. In this lecture we classify dynamical systems which arise from iterating complex analytic self-maps of the Riemann sphere; that is, rational maps.

These systems arise naturally also, in numerical analysis; for example, in root-finding algorithms for polynomials. Recall that if $P(z)$ is a polynomial, Newton's method for finding its roots is as follows. Choose a starting point z_0. Then set

$$z_{n+1} = z_n - \frac{P(z_n)}{P'(z_n)}.$$

For "most" choices of starting point, this iteration will converge to a root of the polynomial; nevertheless, there are many choices of z_0 for which the iteration does not converge at all, but for which the iterates behave chaotically. This dichotomy between predictable and chaotic behavior is typical of dynamical systems determined by rational maps. Newton's method is

1980 *Mathematics Subject Classification* (1985 *Revision*). Primary 30Cxx, 58S11, 65E05.

The author was supported in part oy National Science Foundation grant #DMS-8503015 and the PSC-CUNY Fellowship Award Program.

precisely the iteration of the rational function:

$$N_P(z) = \frac{z P'(z) - P(z)}{P'(z)}.$$

Below, we survey the theory of dynamical systems which arise from iterating an arbitrary rational map. We work only in the dynamical space of a rational map and do not study the dependence on parameters. The question of dependence on parameters will be discussed by Branner in the next lecture. Since the theory is very rich and space here is limited, we give only those proofs which best give the flavor of the subject. The interested reader can pursue further details and history in the bibliography.

1. Background. Let us begin by recalling some basic properties of rational maps. A rational map $R(z)$ of the Riemann sphere is an analytic self map that can be expressed as a quotient of polynomials:

$$R(z) = \frac{P(z)}{Q(z)}, \qquad P(z), Q(z) \not\equiv 0.$$

This quotient is said to be in *lowest terms* if P and Q have no common factors; a lowest terms representation is unique up to multiplication of the numerator and denominator by a nonzero constant.

The most basic invariant of a rational map is its *degree* which can be defined in several ways. The simplest definition is given by:

$$d = \text{degree } R = \max\{\text{degree } P, \text{ degree } Q\}$$

where $R = P/Q$ is a lowest terms representation of R. Equivalently, degree R is the maximum number of distinct preimages of any value. In fact, this maximum is attained at all but a finite number of values.

Other basic concepts involving rational maps are the following:

DEFINITION. R is a local homeomorphism at all but finitely many points; those points where it fails to be a homeomorphism are *critical points*. In a neighborhood of a critical point, R is a k to 1 ramified covering of its image, $k \leq d$.

DEFINITION. A *critical value* is the image of a critical point.

A point has the maximal number of distinct preimages if and only if it is not a critical value. Critical values have fewer preimages and it can be shown by the Riemann-Hurwitz theorem ([**B1**]) that counted properly, a degree d rational map has exactly $2d - 2$ critical values.

DEFINITION. The *orbit* of a point z is the set of forward iterates

$$\{z, R(z), R \circ R(z), R \circ R \circ R(z), \dots\}.$$

DEFINITION. The *post-critical* set is the closure of the set of orbits of the critical points. In the analysis of the dynamical system defined by iterating the map R, the role of the post-critical set is crucial.

Rational maps are complex analytic functions so the theory of one complex variable plays a role in our study. We recall several important facts from this theory.

Let $\Delta = \{z \mid |z| < 1\}$.

LEMMA 1 (SCHWARZ). *Suppose* $f: \Delta \to \Delta$ *is analytic and* $f(0) = 0$. *Then* $|f(z)| \leq |z|$ *for all* $z \in \Delta$ *and* $|f'(0)| \leq 1$. *If equality holds in either case then* $f(z) = \lambda z$, *where* $|\lambda| = 1$.

DEFINITION. The unit disk carries a unique Riemannian metric of constant curvature -1 which is commonly known as the *Poincaré metric*; its density function is given by:

$$\rho_\Delta(z) = 2/(1 - |z|^2).$$

COROLLARY 1. *An analytic map* $f: \Delta \to \Delta$ *is nonexpanding in the Poincaré metric.*

THEOREM 1 (RIEMANN MAPPING). *Every simply connected domain in* $\widehat{\mathbb{C}}$ *with more than two boundary points is conformally equivalent to* Δ.

THEOREM 2 (UNIFORMIZATION THEOREM). *Every simply connected Riemann surface is conformally equivalent to either* $\widehat{\mathbb{C}}, \mathbb{C}$ *or* Δ.

REMARK. Although $\mathbb{C}$ and Δ are topologically equivalent, they are not conformally equivalent—by Liouville's theorem a bounded entire function is constant.

REMARK. To apply the uniformization theorem to an arbitrary Riemann surface S, we apply it to the universal cover of S (which is simply connected). $\widehat{\mathbb{C}}$ is the universal cover only of itself; $\mathbb{C}$ is the universal cover of itself, a cylinder or a torus; Δ is the universal cover for all other Riemann surfaces.

THEOREM 3. *The uniform limit of a uniformly convergent sequence of complex analytic functions is a complex analytic function.*

Note that a constant is an analytic function, and on $\widehat{\mathbb{C}}$, the constant ∞ is allowed.

NOTATION. If R is a rational map, denote by $R^{\circ n}$ the rational map obtained by composing R with itself n times.

EXAMPLE 1. Let $R(z) = z^2$. On any compact subset of Δ, R^n tends uniformly to the constant function 0.

We now recall:

DEFINITION. A family of complex analytic functions $\{f_\alpha\}$, defined on a domain D is called a *normal family* if it satisfies the following condition: every infinite subset of $\{f_\alpha\}$ contains a subsequence which converges uniformly on every compact subset of D.

REMARK. The limit function is generally not a member of the family. In Example 1 above, where the members of the family were the iterates of z^2, the limit function did not belong to the family.

DEFINITION. A family $F = \{f_\alpha\}$ of continuous functions is *equicontinuous* if, given any $\varepsilon > 0$, there is a $\delta = \delta(\varepsilon, z)$, such that $|f_\alpha(z) - f_\alpha(w)| < \varepsilon$, whenever $|z - w| < \delta$.

Two important characterizations of normal families are:

THEOREM 4 (ARZELA-ASCOLI). *A family F is normal on D if and only if it is equicontinuous there.*

THEOREM 5 (MONTEL). *Let F be a family of analytic functions defined on a domain D. If the union $\bigcup_{f \in F} f(D)$ omits three points in $\widehat{\mathbb{C}}$, then F is a normal family.*

2. The basic dichotomy. We can now define the basic dichotomy of $\widehat{\mathbb{C}}$ determined by the rational map R and its iterates $R^{\circ n}(z) = R \circ R \circ \cdots \circ R(z)$.

DEFINITIONS. z is a *stable point* for R if there is a neighborhood U of z on which the iterates R^n form a normal family. Let Ω_R (or Ω if there is no confusion) denote the stable set of R. The *Julia set* or the *unstable set* is the complement of Ω_R; it is denoted J_R (or simply J). It is named after the mathematician Julia who, along with Fatou, began this subject in the 1920's.

The set Ω is open by definition; it must either be empty or dense in $\widehat{\mathbb{C}}$ and it is often not connected. The Julia set is closed and we prove, in Proposition 3, that the dynamical system behaves chaotically there. In Proposition 2, we prove that J is not empty and so always exhibits chaotic dynamics.

We prove easily that Ω_R and J_R are both *completely invariant* under R; that is:

PROPOSITION 1. *If z is in Ω_R, then the image and preimages are also in Ω_R.*

PROOF. Let U be a neighborhood of z on which the iterates $R^{\circ n}$ form a normal family. $R(U)$ is open by the open mapping theorem. If $R^{\circ n_j}$ is a convergent sequence on U, $R^{\circ n_j - 1}$ is a convergent sequence on $R(U)$. Similarly, $R^{-1}(U)$ is open and on each component of $R^{-1}(U)$, $R^{\circ n_j + 1}$ is a convergent sequence.

COROLLARY 2. *J_R is completely invariant.*

PROPOSITION 2. *J is not empty.*

PROOF. Suppose it were. Then, for any point z, we could find a neighborhood U and a subsequence of the iterates $R^{\circ n_j}$ which would converge to an analytic function $\rho: U \to \widehat{\mathbb{C}}$. By the monodromy theorem ρ can be continued analytically to the whole all of $\widehat{\mathbb{C}}$ and therefore is a rational function of degree d, $d < \infty$. Since ρ is the limit of functions whose degrees tend to ∞, it must have degree ∞, contradicting the previous sentence.

EXAMPLE 1 (REVISITED). We saw above that the interior of the disk Δ consists of stable points if $R(z) = z^2$. Similarly the iterates of all points in $\widehat{\mathbb{C}} - \Delta$ tend to ∞; the limit function is the constant ∞, and $\widehat{\mathbb{C}} - \Delta$ also consists of stable points. On the boundary, $|z| = 1$, the situation is different. The circle is completely invariant; any neighborhood U of a point on the circle is expanded by R, and as we will see later, the union of its iterates, $\bigcup_n R^{\circ n}(U)$, covers all points in $\widehat{\mathbb{C}}$ except 0 and ∞. Montel's theorem implies the circle is the Julia set.

FIGURE 1. Filled Julia set of $z^2 + c$ where $c = -0.12256117 + .74486177i$ ("Douady's Rabbit"—Superattractive Cycle).

FIGURE 2. Blow up of the marked area in Figure 1— quasi-self similarity.

Figures 1 and 2 illustrate the filled Julia sets of some other quadratic polynomials—the Julia set is the boundary of the black region. See also Color Plates 1–12.

As mentioned above, J may be the whole sphere. This is the case for the function $R(z) = (z - 2)^2/z^2$ first considered by Guckenheimer. We will understand why later.

Note that $R^{\circ k}$ is a rational map of degree d^k. It is clear from the definition that $\Omega_{R^{\circ k}} = \Omega_R$ and therefore that $J_{R^{\circ k}} = J_R$.

If $z \in J$, there is no neighborhood U of z on which the iterates of R form a normal family. By Montel's theorem, $\bigcup_n R^{\circ n}(U) \supset \hat{\mathbb{C}} - E$, where E is a completely invariant set containing 0, 1 or 2 points; E is called the *exceptional set*.

Suppose E contains 1 point, $E = \{e\}$. Since E is invariant, e is a point of multiplicity d. If $e = \infty$, R is a polynomial. Otherwise, R is conjugate to a polynomial by the fractional linear map $w(z) = 1/(z - e)$. We will see below that ∞ is always a stable point for a polynomial.

Next suppose E contains 2 points, $E = \{a, b\}$. Conjugating R by the linear fractional transformation $w = (z - a)/(z - b)$, if necessary, we can assume that $E = \{0, \infty\}$. Since E is invariant, R either fixes 0 and ∞, or it interchanges them. If it fixes them, $R(\infty) = \infty$, $R(0) = 0$, then both points are of multiplicity d and the only function R can be is $R = z^d$. On the other hand, if $R(0) = \infty$, the only possibility is $R = z^{-d}$. We will see below that J_R is the unit circle in either of these cases and that 0 and ∞ are stable points. In all other cases E is empty.

Suppose z is stable and w is nearby. Then w is stable and if $R^{\circ n_j}(z) \to p(z)$, p extends to a function defined at w and $R^{\circ n_j}(w) \to p(w)$. For example, if the Newton rational map is converging to a root for some initial guess, it will converge to the same root for a nearby initial guess. On the other hand, if z is unstable, and w is a nearby unstable point, knowing the orbit of z gives us no information at all about the orbit of w. That is, the dynamical system restricted to J has sensitive dependence on initial parameters. This is stated explicitly in:

PROPOSITION 3. *If $w \in J$, $\bigcup_n R^{\circ -n}(w)$ is dense in J.*

PROOF. Let U be a neighborhood of w. If $z \in J$, there is some k so that $z \in R^{\circ k}(U)$; therefore, for some branch of $R^{\circ -k}$, $R^{\circ -k}(z) \in U$.

REMARK. This proof actually shows more. It shows that if z is not in the exceptional set E, then the inverse images, $R^{\circ -n}(z)$, accumulate onto the Julia set. It is this property of the Julia set which is used most often in creating the computer pictures which approximate the Julia sets of quadratic polynomials.

PROPOSITION 4. *J is an infinite set (hence by the above, it is perfect).*

The proposition follows from the following lemma:

LEMMA 2. *If S is a nonempty completely invariant set under the rational map R, then it contains one, two or infinitely many points.*

PROOF. Suppose S contains finitely many points, $S = \{a_0, a_1, \ldots, a_k\}$. Since S is completely invariant, there is some power of R which fixes each point in S; that is, $R^{\circ p}(a_i) = a_i$, $i = 0, \ldots, k$. To simplify notation, let d be the degree of $R^{\circ p}$.

Now, the complete invariance implies that each point of this set has only itself as preimage under $R^{\circ p}$ and therefore each of these points is critical with multiplicity $d - 1$. Since the total number of critical points counted with multiplicities is $2d - 2$, k is at most 2.

PROOF OF PROPOSITION 4. Recall our discusson of exceptional sets above. A completely invariant set containing only one or two points must be the exceptional set of a polynomial. We will show below, In our classification of stable regions, that points in the exceptional set are always stable; therefore, the nonempty, completely invariant set J must contain infinitely many points.

PROPOSITION 5. *There is no closed completely invariant set properly contained in J.*

PROOF. Suppose $K \subset J$ is closed and completely invariant. If $w \in K$, the inverse orbit of w is dense in J and belongs to K by the invariance of J. Since K is closed $K = J$.

PROPOSITION 6. *If J contains a nonempty open subset of $\widehat{\mathbb{C}}$, $J = \widehat{\mathbb{C}}$.*

PROOF. Let U be an open set in the interior of J. By Montel's theorem, $\bigcup_n R^{\circ n}(U) \supset \widehat{\mathbb{C}} - E$. By the invariance of J, $J \supset \widehat{\mathbb{C}} - E$. Since J is closed and E contains at most 2 points, $J = \widehat{\mathbb{C}}$.

3. Periodic points. A *period-p periodic cycle* of points is a sequence of distinct points, $\{z_0, z_1, \ldots, z_{p-1}\}$ such that $z_i = R(z_{i-1})$ and $z_0 = R(z_{p-1})$. From the chain rule, it follows that the same value is obtained by evaluating the derivative $(R^{\circ p})'$ at each of the z_i's; this common value, λ, is the *eigenvalue* of the cycle.

DEFINITION. A periodic point or cycle is called

attracting if	$0 < |\lambda| < 1$
super-attracting if	$|\lambda| = 0$
repelling if	$|\lambda| > 1$
neutral if	$|\lambda| = 1$.

PROPOSITION 7 (POINCARÉ LINEARIZATION). *Suppose z_0 is an attracting periodic point of period p and eigenvalue λ. Then there exists a neighborhood U of z_0 and a complex analytic map $\varphi : U \to \Delta$ such that $\varphi(z_0) = 0$ and*

$$(*) \qquad \qquad \varphi \circ R^{\circ p}(z) = \lambda\varphi(z).$$

φ is said to linearize $R^{\circ p}$ in U.

SKETCH OF PROOF. We apply the standard method of undetermined coefficients. Assume φ exists. Since it is analytic, it has a power series expansion about z_0. The equation $(*)$ puts a recursive constraint on the coefficients of φ. These conditions imply that the series actually converges and is not just a formal power series.

COROLLARY 3. *If z_0 is a repelling periodic point and $(R^{\circ p}(z_0))' = \lambda$, there exist neighborhoods U' and U, $U' \subset U$, and an analytic conjugation $\varphi: U \to \Delta$ such that $\varphi(z_0) = 0$, and*

$$
\begin{array}{ccc}
U' & \overset{R^{\circ p}}{\to} & U \\
\varphi \downarrow & & \downarrow \varphi \\
\Delta & \overset{\lambda z}{\to} & \Delta.
\end{array}
$$

REMARK. Since U' is mapped outside itself, this process cannot be iterated.

PROOF. Apply the previous argument to the branch of $R^{\circ p-1}$ which fixes z_0.

PROPOSITION 8. *If z_0 is a super-attracting periodic point of period p, there exists a neighborhood U of z_0 and a function $\varphi: U \to \Delta$ such that if the first $k - 1$ derivatives of $R^{\circ p}$ vanish at z_0, then $\varphi \circ R^{\circ p} = (\varphi(z))^k$.*

PROOF. Essentially the same as the contracting case.

THEOREM 6 (SCHROEDER). *A fixed point is stable if and only if there is an analytic conjugacy to a linear map in a neighborhood of the point.*

It follows that attracting and super-attracting periodic points are stable and that repelling periodic points are unstable. If the periodic point is neutral, the situation is more delicate and will be discussed in the next section.

We come now to a fundamental characterization of Julia sets—the Julia set is the closure of the repelling periodic points. The proof of the analogous statement for real polynomials using symbolic dynamics does not work here. We give the proof for a large and important class of rational maps, *expanding maps*.

DEFINITION. *R is expanding if its Julia set is disjoint from the closure of the forward orbits of the critical points.*

PROPOSITION 9. *The Julia set is the closure of the repelling periodic points.*

PROOF (in the expanding case only). Let $w \in J$, and choose a neighborhood U of w, disjoint from the closure of the post-critical set. There is an integer k, such that $R^{\circ k}(U) \supset U$, and since there are no critical points of $R^{\circ k}$ in U, there is a well-defined branch of $R^{\circ -k}$ such that $V = R^{\circ -k}(U) \subset U$. By the corollary to the Schwarz lemma, $R^{\circ -nk}(U), n > 0$, form a nested sequence; their intersection contains an attracting fixed point z_0 for $R^{\circ -k}$. It is the required repelling periodic point for R.

COROLLARY 4. *If D is a domain which intersects J, then there is an integer k such that $R^{\circ k}$ maps $D \cap J$ onto J.*

PROOF. Let $v \in D \cap J$ be a repelling periodic point and let U be a neighborhood of v which is mapped strictly over itself by $R^{\circ k}$ for some k; $U \subset R^{\circ k}(U)$. Consider the nested sequence $R^{\circ nk}(U), n > 0$. Since $J = J_R = J_{R^{\circ k}}, v \in J_{R^{\circ k}}$, and $\bigcup_n R^{\circ nk}(U) \supset J$. The compactness of J in $\widehat{\mathbb{C}}$ implies there is some N such that $J \subset \bigcup_1^N R^{\circ nk}(U)$.

Corollary 4 says that a small piece of the Julia set is eventually mapped onto the whole Julia set by some iterate of the map; this is a property enjoyed by self-similar sets. Now a Julia set is rarely self-similar, however the Julia set of an expanding map has a very useful property which is weaker than self-similarity. To describe this property we need some definitions.

DEFINITION. A map $F: X \rightarrow Y$ from a metric space X with metric d to itself is a K-*quasi-isometry* if

$$\frac{1}{K}d(x,y) < d(F(x), F(y)) < Kd(x,y)$$

for all x, y in X.

NOTATION. $\varphi_r(x) = (1/r)x$ is the stretch by $1/r$; $B_r(x_0)$ is the disk of radius r centered at x_0.

DEFINITION. A set S in X is K-*quasi-self-similar* if there exists a K and an r_0 such that

$$\varphi_r(S \cap B_r(x))$$

can be mapped onto S by a K-quasi-isometry for all x in S and all $r < r_0$.

THEOREM 7 (SULLIVAN [Sul3]). *The Julia set of an expanding rational map is* K-*quasi-self-similar for some* K.

Figures 1 and 2 show the quasi-self-similarity. Also see Color Plates 1, 2, 3, 5 and 6. The map in Color Plates 7, 8 and 9 is not expanding, although the figures indicate quasi-self-similarity.

4. Classification of stable domains. We say in §2 that the stable set Ω of R is open, and it is easy to see that if D_0 is a maximal connected component of Ω, then $R(D_0)$ is a component as well. Now D_0 must be one of two types:

  (i) either the forward iterates $R^{\circ j}(D_0)$ are disjoint, in which case D_0 is *wandering*, or
  (ii) there exist integers $m, n \geq 0$ such that $R^{\circ n}(D_0) = R^{\circ m}(D_0)$, and D_0 is *eventually periodic*.

The qualitative and quantitative classification of eventually periodic domains was begun by Fatou and Julia and was completed by Siegel, Herman, Sullivan and Shishikura. We summarize it below. Complete details and proofs are in Fatou [F1], Sullivan [Sul1, Sul3], Siegel [Si], Herman [H1, H2], Camacho [Ca] and Shishikura [Shi]. A more detailed survey is in Blanchard [Bl].

In the early 1980's Sullivan ruled out case (ii) using sophisticated techniques borrowed from Teichmüller theory.

THEOREM 8 (SULLIVAN [Sul1]). *Every component of the stable set of a rational map is eventually periodic.*

In view of Theorem 8 there is a natural partition of the set of components of the stable set into equivalence classes given by: $U \approx V$ if U and V eventually fall into the same periodic cycle. Therefore the number of equivalence classes equals the number of periodic cycles. It was known classically that this number is bounded in terms of the degree of the map. A recent theorem of Shishikura gives a sharp upper bound.

THEOREM 9 (SHISHIKURA). *A degree d rational map has at most $2d - 2$ cycles of periodic stable domains.*

Up to analytic conjugacy there are five distinct models for the first return map of a periodic cycle. To describe them requires some definitions.

DEFINITION. The *attractive basin* of a periodic cycle is the set of points whose orbits tend to the cycle.

DEFINITION. The *immediate attractive basin* of a periodic cycle is the set of components of the attractive basin which contain the cycle.

DEFINITION. Let z and w be points in $\widehat{\mathbb{C}}$. Then z and w are *grand orbit equivalent, $z \sim w$,* if there are integers m and n such that $R^{\circ m}(z) = R^{\circ n}(w)$.

Model 1: Attractive cycles.

PROPOSITION 10. *The immediate attractive basin of an attractive periodic cycle contains at least one critical point.*

PROOF (in the fixed point case only). Let z_0 be an attracting fixed point and denote the immediate attractive basin of z_0 by $I(z_0)$. If z_0 is a super-attractive fixed point, it is already a critical point.

Suppose the eigenvalue λ at z_0 is not 0. Let $I = I(z_0) - \{\text{grand orbit of } z_0\}$. Using the analytic conjugacy of Proposition 7 one shows that the projection onto the quotient of I by the grand orbit equivalency, $p: I \to I/ \sim$ is an analytic map onto a torus T. Since I contains more than three boundary points, the uniformization theorem implies there is a universal covering map, $\pi: \Delta \to I$. If I contains no critical points, the composition $p \circ \pi$ is a universal covering map of the torus T by the unit disk contradicting the uniformization theorem.

COROLLARY 5. *There are at most $2d - 2$ attracting (or super-attracting) periodic cycles.*

Model 2: Super-attractive cycles. In the attractive basin of a super-attractive periodic point, there is a dynamically defined foliation invariant under R. By Proposition 8, the first return map is conjugate to $z \to z^d$ near the periodic point and the inverse images of the circles $|z| = r$ define the foliation.

Model 3: Parabolic cycles. A *parabolic cycle* is the immediate attractive basin of a periodic point whose eigenvalue is a root of unity. The points in the periodic cycle are in J for if they were stable, the first return map would be conjugate to the identity in each component of the cycle.

In the neighborhood of a parabolic periodic point, the dynamics are described by Camacho in his " Flower Theorem" ([Ca]). Briefly, the neighborhood is divided into sectors (the number of sectors depends on the first

FIGURE 3. Filled Julia set of $z^2 - \frac{3}{4}$ with parabolic cycle.

return map at the point); each component of the immediate attractive basin of the point is in one sector. (See Figure 3 where there are two sectors.) The fixed point is an attractor for points in these components.

PROPOSITION 11. *The immediate attractive basin of a parabolic periodic cycle contains a critical point.*

PROOF (again in the case of a parabolic fixed point). We argue as in the proof of Proposition 10. The quotient of the immediate basin of attraction I by the grand orbit relation is a covering map of a twice punctured sphere S_2. If there were no critical points, the projection of I onto S_2 composed with the universal covering of I would be a universal covering of S_2, contradicting the uniformization theorem.

Model 4: Siegel disks. A *Siegel disk* is a component D of Ω_R such that:

(i) D contains a periodic point
(ii) the first return map fixing D is conjugate to an irrational rotation of the disk Δ.

This conjugation determines a foliation of D by the inverse images of the circles in Δ. This is similar to the super-attractive model, however, in the Siegel disk each leaf is mapped one to one onto itself by the first return map.

Siegel [Si] gave a sufficient condition for this conjugation to exist.

DEFINITION. The number α is *diophantine* if there exist $c > 0$ and $\nu > 0$ such that for every rational number p/q (in lowest terms)

$$|\alpha - p/q| > c/q^{\nu}.$$

THEOREM 10 (SIEGEL). *A sufficient condition for the first return map at a periodic cycle to be conjugate to an irrational rotation is that the eigenvalue at the cycle be of the form:*

$$\lambda = \exp(2\pi i\alpha) \text{ where } \alpha \text{ is diophantine.}$$

There are examples of neutral periodic cycles with $\lambda = \exp(2\pi i\alpha)$ and α irrational but not diophantine, found by Cremer [**Cr**], for which this conjugacy cannot exist. They are chosen so that there are periodic points in any neighborhood of the cycle. Necessary and sufficient conditions for the conjugacy to exist are not known.

Fatou and Julia proved that the boundaries of stable periodic components containing a neutral periodic cycle are contained in the accumulation set of the post-critical set.

See Figure 4 for an example of a Siegel disk in the family $z \to z^2 + c$.

FIGURE 4. Filled Julia set of $z^2 - \lambda z, \lambda = .7373688 + 0.6754903i$-cycle of Siegel disks.

Model 5: Herman rings. A *Herman ring* is a component of the stable set which is topologically an annulus and on which the first return map is analytically conjugate to an irrational rotation of a regular annulus.

The inverse images of the circles in the regular annulus form an invariant foliation of the Herman ring. It is clear that the ring contains no periodic point. The proof that the boundary of the Herman ring is contained in the accumulation set of the orbits of the critical points is the same as it is for Siegel disks.

Examples were found by Michel Herman in the family

$$z \to \frac{e^{i\alpha}}{z} \left(\frac{z-a}{1-az} \right)^2$$

for α diophantine and a chosen properly. The restriction of a map in this family to the unit circle S^1 is a rotation, and each hemisphere surjects onto $\widehat{\mathbb{C}}$.

To summarize:

THEOREM 11. *Each eventually periodic component of Ω lands on one of*: *attractive cycle, super-attractive cycle, parabolic cycle, Siegel disk or Herman ring.*

COROLLARY 6. *If every critical point is preperiodic, and no critical point is periodic then $J = \widehat{\mathbb{C}}$.*

PROOF. Each type of stable domain except a super-attracting one requires an infinite critical orbit; a super-attracting stable domain has only a periodic critical point.

We can now prove that in Guckenheimer's example, $R(z) = (z-2)^2/z^2$, the stable set is empty and $J = \widehat{\mathbb{C}}$. The critical points are at $z = 2$ and $z = \infty$. Computing critical orbits we have:

$$2 \to 0 \to \infty \to 1 \to 1,$$

so Corollary 6 applies.

Theorem 11 implies that expanding rational maps have only attracting and super-attracting behavior.

5. Connectivity. In Example 1 the stable set has two connected components. Each is completely invariant under the map R. If D is any completely invariant component of the stable set, ∂D is completely invariant also. Since $J \supset \partial D$ and J is the smallest closed invariant set, $J = \partial D$.

PROPOSITION 12. *There are at most two distinct completely invariant components of Ω.*

IDEA OF PROOF. The boundary of any completely invariant component is the entire Julia set; this fact together with a study of the deployment of the critical points implies there are only two.

Proposition 12 implies:

PROPOSITION 13. *If the number of components of Ω is finite, it is at most two.*

PROOF. If there are only finitely many components, each is completely in-variant under some iterate and they are all completely invariant by a suitably high iterate. By Proposition 12 there are at most two.

EXAMPLE 2. Let $R(z) = z^2 - 2$. Since R is a polynomial, ∞ is stable and is contained in a superattractive stable domain D. The critical point 0 is preperiodic and not periodic; $0 \to -2 \to -2$, hence R has no other stable domains. D is completely invariant and the only component of Ω. J is the real interval $[-2, 2]$.

If R is a polynomial whose finite critical points are all preperiodic but not periodic, J_R is called a *dendrite*. Example 2 is one such polynomial. Another example is $R(z) = z^2 + i$. (See Figure 5.)

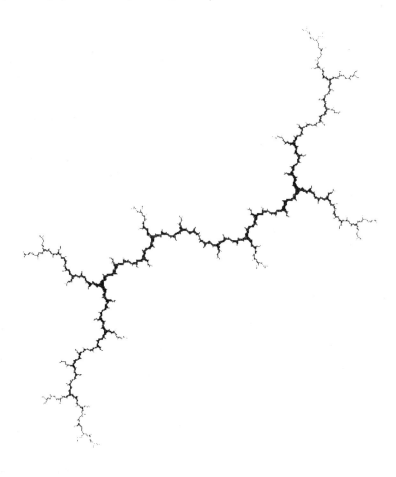

FIGURE 5. Julia set of $z^2 + i$—"Dendrite."

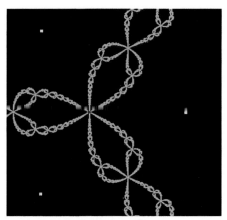

COLOR PLATE 1

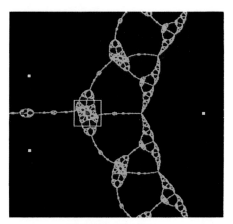

COLOR PLATE 2

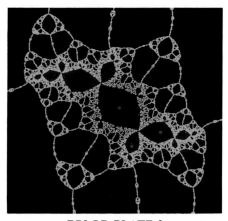

COLOR PLATE 3

Color Plates 1–6 show the iteration procedure for Newton's method for a cubic polynomial. In Color Plate 1, the polynomial is $z^3 - 1$; in Color Plate 2, the polynomial is in the center of the 3-ball of the Mandelbrot set in Color Plate 12 of Branner's article. Color Plate 3 is a blow up of the indicated area in Color Plate 2. Note the "rabbits" in this picture; the critical point has period 6 and bounces around in two rabbits.

COLOR PLATE 4

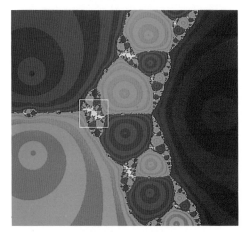

COLOR PLATE 5

COLOR PLATE 6

Color Plates 4, 5, and 6 show filled in Julia sets colored to show the different basins of attraction of the roots. The yellow sets are points that are not attracted to roots. Compare Color Plates 1 and 4, 2 and 5, and 3 and 6.

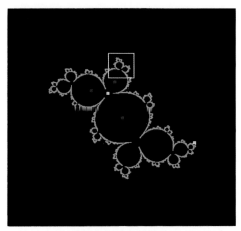

COLOR PLATE 7

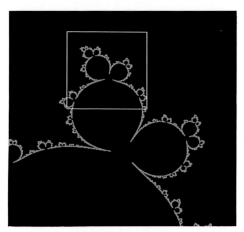

COLOR PLATE 8

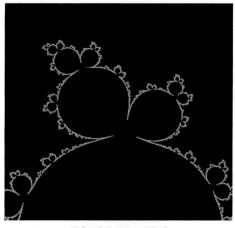

COLOR PLATE 9

Color Plates 7–12 show the iteration of a quadratic polynomial $z^2 + c$. Color Plate 7 is the Julia set for a parabolic cycle of period 3—the "fat rabbit"—with $c = -.1250000 + .649519i$. Color Plates 8 and 9 are successive blow ups of the Julia set in Color Plate 7.

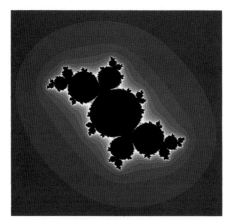

COLOR PLATE 10

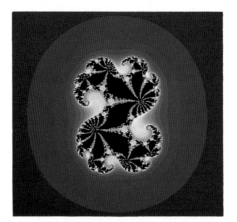

COLOR PLATE 11

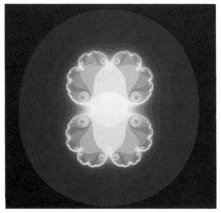

COLOR PLATE 12

Color Plate 10 *is the filled in Julia set for the "fat rabbit." The level curves of the escape rate are visible. Color Plate* 11 *is the filled Julia set for the polynomial with super-attractive periodic cycle of period* 12, *the center of the main component in Color Plate* 9 *of Branner's article. Color Plate* 12 *shows the escape rates colored for a polynomial with Julia set a Cantor set;* $c = .3000$.

EXAMPLE 3. The map $R(z) = z^2 + c$, where $(c^2 + c)^2 + c = 0$, has 0 as a super-attractive periodic point. The immediate basin at 0 contains three distinct components; by Proposition 13 there are infinitely many distinct components. (See Figure 1.)

EXAMPLE 4. Let $R(z) = z^2 + 3$. The critical value is $c = 3$. It is easy to see that the orbit of the critical value, $3 \rightarrow 12 \rightarrow 147 \rightarrow \ldots$ tends to the super-attractive fixed point ∞. The map R is expanding and the stable set is the immediate attracting basin of ∞; it consists of all points which tend to ∞. The Julia set is the set of points which don't go to ∞. To find its structure, set $\Gamma = \{z \mid |z| = 2.5\}$. The orbit of any point outside Γ goes to ∞. Γ contains two preimages of itself, Γ_0 and Γ_1, which are disjoint and don't contain the critical point 0. (See Figure 6.) The region bounded by the three curves is mapped outside Γ so all points in it have orbits which go to ∞. Continue taking preimages of Γ and labelling them: $\Gamma_{00}, \Gamma_{01}, \Gamma_{10}, \Gamma_{11}$, etc. The Julia set is a Cantor set in the intersection of these preimages. The stable set is the complement of this Cantor set and is infinitely connected. (See Color Plate 12.)

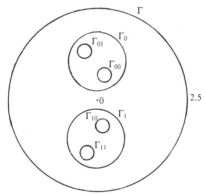

FIGURE 6. Construction of Julia set of $z^2 + 3$—Cantor set construction.

PROPOSITION 14. *If R is a polynomial, all the bounded components of the stable set are simply connected.*

IDEA OF PROOF. Suppose D is a multiply connected bounded component. D is fixed by the first return map. Let Γ be a curve which contains a bounded component B, of the complement of D. Since B contains no poles, the iterates of the first return map R at any point in B can be expressed in terms of Cauchy's integral formula. From the formula we conclude that these iterates are bounded in B so B contains no unstable points.

Proposition 14 clearly isn't true for rational maps; for example, those with Herman rings. These are the only possible domains of finite nonzero connectivity. This follows from Theorem 10 and

PROPOSITION 15. *The connectivity of any component of the immediate basin of an attracting or parabolic cycle is either 0 or infinity.*

PROOF (in the attracting case). Let z_0 be an attracting periodic point of R, and I the component of the immediate basin of attraction which contains it. Now z_0 is a fixed point of the first return map, $R^{\circ p}$. Let U_0 be a neighborhood of z_0 on which the first return map can be linearized. Inductively, set

$$U_n = (R^{\circ p})^{-1}(U_{n-1}) \cap I.$$

The U_n form an increasing nested sequence whose union is I. If I is not simply connected, some U_k is already not simply connected and has at least two boundary components. Since the degree of R is at least two, the number of boundary components of each succeeding U_{n+k} is at least doubled. I is therefore infinitely connected. (Compare Example 4.)

6. Open problems. (1) It is not hard to prove that if R is expanding the measure of its Julia set is zero. Computer pictures indicate that this should be true for an arbitrary rational map—find a proof. See Harrison's article and the references there.

(2) Can the Hausdorff measure of the Julia set of a rational map be 2? Again see Harrison's article in this volume.

(3) Computer pictures indicate that the Julia set of an arbitrary rational map is quasi-self-similar—find a proof. See [Sul2].

(4) The rotation domains are the least understood of the stable domains. A particular problem is to study the topological deployment of the Herman rings. Some work has been done by Douady and Shishikura using "surgery" techniques; they build up rational maps from stable cycles of various different rational maps. See [Do2], [M] and [Shi].

(5) The relationship between the arithmetic properties of the eigenvalue λ of a neutral periodic cycle and its stability are not fully understood. See [Cr] and [H1].

(6) The boundary of a rotation domain contains the accumulation set of the post critical set. For a Siegel disk in the family $z \to z^2 + c$, the critical point itself is always in the boundary. Is this true for an arbitrary rotation domain? See [H2].

(7) Does the rational map R act ergodically on its Julia set? See [GGS] and [R].

(8) We have described the connectivity properties of the stable domains. This doesn't, however, give us information on the local connectivity of the Julia set. Computer experiments for quadratic polynomials show that their Julia sets are probably locally connected. Prove some statements about local connectivity of the Julia set. See [Sul2], Branner's article in this volume and the references therein.

The author would like to thank Lisa R. Goldberg for her comments and suggestions during the preparation of this article. She would also like to thank Wei-Hua Jiang for creating the computer pictures in the text. Thanks are also due to Homer Smith for providing the Color Plates 1–12.

REFERENCES

[A1] L. Ahlfors, *Complex analysis*, McGraw-Hill, 1979.

[A2] L. Ahlfors, *Conformal invariants. Topics in geometric function theory*, McGraw-Hill, 1973.

[A3] L. Ahlfors and L. Bers, *Riemann's mapping theorem for variable metrics*, Ann. of Math. (2) **72** (1960), 385–404.

[Ba1] I. N. Baker, *Repulsive fixpoints of entire functions*, Math. Z. **104** (1968), 252–256.

[Ba2] I. N. Baker, *The domains of normality of an entire function*, Ann. Acad. Sci. Fenn. Ser A I Math. **1** (1975), 277–283.

[Ba3] I. N. Baker, *Wandering domains in the iteration of entire functions*, Proc. London Math. Soc. **49** (1984), 563–576.

[Ba4] I. N. Baker, *Limit functions and sets of non-normality in iteration theory*, Ann. Acad. Sci. Fenn. (A) **467** (1970), 1–11.

[Ba5] I. N. Baker, *Fixpoints of polynomials and rational functions*, J. London Math. Soc. **39** (1964), 615–622.

[Ba6] I. N. Baker, *The iteration of polynomials and transcendental entire functions*, J. Austral. Math. Soc. (A) **30** (1981), 483–495.

[Ba7] I. N. Baker, *The distribution of fixpoints of entire functions*, Proc. London Math. Soc. (3) **16** (1966), 493–506.

[Be] L. Bers, *On Sullivan's proof of the finiteness theorem and the eventual periodicity theorem*, Amer. J. Math. **109** (1987), 833–852.

[BH] B. Branner, and J. Hubbard, *The iteration of cubic polynomials, part 1: the global topology of parameter space*, Acta Math. (to appear).

[Bl] P. Blanchard, *Complex analytic dynamics on the Riemann sphere*, Bull. Amer. Math. Soc. (N.S.) **11** (1984), 85–141.

[Br] H. Brolin, *Invariant sets under iteration of rational functions*, Ark. Mat. **6** (1965), 103–144.

[Bra] B. Branner, *Mandelbrot sets*, this volume.

[Ca] C. Camacho, *On the local structure of conformal mappings and holomorphic vector fields*, Astérisque **59–60** (1978), 83–94.

[Cr] H. Cremer, *Zum Zentrumproblem*, Math. Ann. **98** (1928), 151–163.

[D] R. L. Devaney, *An introduction to chaotic dynamical systems*, Addison-Wesley, 1987.

[DK] R. L. Devaney, and M. Krych, *Dynamics of* exp(z), J. Ergodic Theory and Dynamical Systems **4** (1984), 35–52.

[DGH] R. L. Devaney, L. R. Goldberg, and J. H. Hubbard, *Dynamics of the exponential map* (preprint).

[DKn] R. L. Devaney and L. Keen, *Dynamics of meromorphic maps: maps with polynomial Schwarzian derivative*, Ann. Sci. École Norm. Sup. (to appear).

[DH1] A. Douady and J. H. Hubbard, *Iteration des polynomes quadratiques complexes*, C. R. Acad. Sci. **294** (1982), 123–126.

[DH2] A. Douady and J. Hubbard, *On the dynamics of polynomial-like mappings*, Ann. Sci. École Norm. Sup. (4) **18** (1985), 287–343.

[DH3] A. Douady and J. H. Hubbard, *Etudes dynamiques des polynomes complexes, avec la collaboration de P. Lavours, Tan Lei and P. Santenac*. I and II, Publ. Math. Orsay, 1985.

[Do1] A. Douady, *Systems dynamiques holomorphes*, Seminaire Bourbaki, 35e annee, 1982–3, 599 Nov 1982.

[Do2] A. Douady, *Chirurgie sur les applications holomorphes*, Proc. ICM86, Proc. Intl. Congress (1986), pp. 724–738.

[E] A. Eremenko, *Iteratsiitzenih funktsii*, Har'kov, 1984.

[F1] P. Fatou, *Sur les equations fonctionnelles*, Bull. Soc. Math. France **47** (1919), 161–271, **48** (1920), 33–34, 208–314.

[F2] P. Fatou, *Sur l'iteration des fonctions transcendentes entieres*, Acta Math. **47** (1920), 337–370.

[GK] L. R. Goldberg and L. Keen, *A finiteness theorem for a dynamical class of entire functions*, J. Ergodic Theory and Dynamical Systems **6** (1986), 183–192.

[Gu] J. Guckenheimer, *Endomorphisms of the Riemann sphere*, Proc. Sympos. Pure Math., vol. 14, Amer. Math. Soc., Providence, RI, 1970.

[GGS] E. Ghys, L. Goldberg, and D. Sullivan, *On the measurable dynamics of $z \to \exp(z)$*, J. Ergodic Theory and Dynamical Systems **5** (1985), pp. 329–335.

[H] J. Harrison, *An introduction to fractals*, this volume.

[H1] M. Herman, *Sur la conjugasion différentiable des diffeomorphismes du cercle des rotations*, Publ. I.H.E.S. **49** (1979), 5–233.

[H2] M. Herman, *Are there critical points on the boundary of singular domains?*, Comm. Math. Phys. **99** (1985), 593–612.

[Ju] G. Julia, *Memoire sur l'iteration des fonctions rationnelles*, J. Math. **8** (1918), 47–245.

[Kn1] L. Keen, *Dynamics of holomorphic maps of C^**, in Holomorphic Functions and Moduli, ed. D. Drasin, Springer, 1988, Proc. Workshop on Holo. Functions and Moduli, MSRI 1986.

[Kn2] L. Keen, *Topology and growth of a special class of holomorphic self-maps of C^**, J. Ergodic Theory and Dynamical Systems (to appear).

[L] S. V. F. Levy, *Critically finite rational maps*, Thesis, Princeton University, 1985.

[M] R. Mane, *On the instability of Herman rings*, Invent. Math. **81** (1985), 459–471.

[MSS] R. Mane, P. Sad and D. Sullivan, *On the dynamics of rational maps*, Ann. Sci. École Norm. Sup. (4) **1** (1985).

[Mc1] C. McMullen, *Area and Hausdorff dimension of Julia sets of entire functions*, Trans. Amer. Math. Soc. **300** (1987), 329–342.

[Mc2] C. McMullen, *Automorphisms of rational maps*, in Holomorphic Functions and Moduli, ed D. Drasin, Springer, 1988.

[R] M. Rees, *Hyperbolic rational maps of degree two*, I (preprint).

[Shi] M. Shishikura, *On the quasiconformal surgery of rational functions*, Ann. Sci. École Norm. Sup. (4) **20** (1987), 1–29.

[Si] C. L. Siegel, *Bermerkung zu einem Satz von Jakob Nielsen*, in Gesammelte Abhandlungen, Vol. 3, Springer-Verlag, 1966, pp. 92, 96.

[Sul1] D. Sullivan, *Quasiconformal homeomorphisms and dynamics*, Annals. Math. **122** (1985), pp. 401–418.

[Sul2] D. Sullivan, *Seminair on conformal and hyperbolic geometry*, IHES Seminar Notes, March, 1982.

[Sul3] D. Sullivan, *Quasiconformal homeomorphisms and dynamics III* (preprint).

[Sul4] D. Sullivan, *Quasiconformal homeomorphisms in dynamics, topology and geometry*, Proc. ICM86, Intl. Congress Math. pp. 1216–1228.

[Y] J.-C. Yoccoz, *Sur la taille des membres de l'ensemble de Mandelbrot*, manuscript, 1986.

DEPARTMENT OF MATHEMATICS, HERBERT H. LEHMAN COLLEGE, CITY UNIVERSITY OF NEW YORK, BRONX, NEW YORK 10468

Proceedings of Symposia in Applied Mathematics
Volume **39**, 1989

The Mandelbrot Set

BODIL BRANNER

1. Introduction. The Mandelbrot set M is defined as the set of $c \in \mathbf{C}$ for which the sequence c, $c^2 + c$, $(c^2 + c)^2 + c, \ldots$ does *not* tend to ∞ as n tends to ∞:

$$M = \{c \in \mathbf{C} | c, c^2 + c, (c^2 + c)^2 + c, \ldots \nrightarrow \infty\}.$$

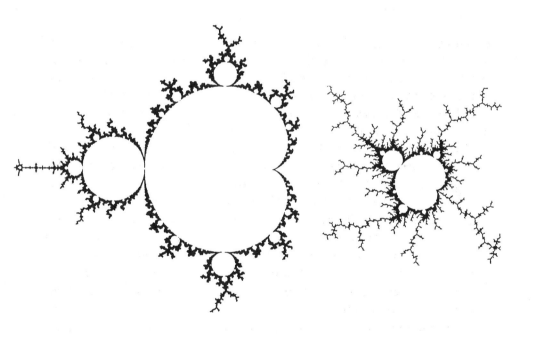

FIGURE 1   FIGURE 2

Figure 1 shows the boundary of M. The set M is extremely complicated. For instance, M contains small copies of itself (see Figure 2) which in turn

---

1980 *Mathematics Subject Classification* (1985 *Revision*). Primary 58F08; Secondary 30D05.

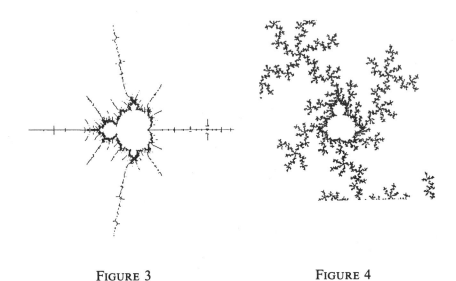

FIGURE 3   FIGURE 4

contain smaller copies of M, and so on ad infinitum. This observation might
lead to the wrong conclusion that the Mandelbrot set M is self-similar. Actually, every mini-Mandelbrot set has its very own pattern of external decorations, every one different from every other (compare Figures 2, 3 and 4
and the Colored Plates 3 and 6). In this paper we shall describe how we can
attempt to understand M (almost completely).

The set M can be defined using nothing more than complex arithmetic,
and not even that if we translate the formula above into real numbers. But
it cannot be understood outside of its context:

Quadratic polynomials as dynamical systems.

To study a polynomial P as a dynamical system, we choose seeds z_0 and
try to understand the long term behaviour of the sequence $z_1 = P(z_0)$, $z_2 = P(z_1), \ldots$. More particularly we will try to answer such questions as:

For a fixed polynomial P what seeds z_0 lead to bounded sequences?

For a parametrized family of polynomials how do the set of such seeds
depend on the parameter?

In most families of dynamical systems there is no obvious picture to make
in the parameter space, since there is no obvious question to ask. The study
of the dynamics of complex polynomials and rational functions is a success
story, mainly because we know which questions to ask:

What happens to the critical points under iteration?

and because we can take advantage of the power of complex analysis. The
Mandelbrot set is an answer to the question above for the complex one-
parameter family of quadratic polynomials $\{P_c\}_{c \in \mathbb{C}}$ where $P_c(z) = z^2 + c$.

The study of quadratic polynomials is fundamental in the following sense. Sets remarkably similar to the Mandelbrot set occur in many other complex one-parameter families of complex analytic mappings. The reason is exactly the same as the reason for why M contains small copies of itself: the mappings, or some iterates thereof, may locally behave like a quadratic polynomial. We say that the Mandelbrot set is a universal object.

The study of analytic mappings under iteration goes back to A. Cayley [C], who at the end of the last century studied Newton's iteration in the complex. In the beginning of this century, up to about 1930, P. Fatou [F] and G. Julia [J] studied iteration of polynomials and rational functions of degree $d \geq 2$. During the next 50 years some papers were published. We only mention the papers by C. Siegel [Si] and H. Brolin [Br]. The subject came back to life with the possibility of computer experiments. To our knowledge the first computer drawing of what came to be called the Mandelbrot set was made in the spring of 1979 by R. Brooks and P. Matelski [BM] when studying discrete subgroups of PSL(2, C). Independently and at about the same time Benoit B. Mandelbrot made computer drawings of the same object [Ma]. That the Mandelbrot set is so well understood is primarily due to the pioneering work in the eighties by A. Douady and J. H. Hubbard (who named the object after Mandelbrot) and D. Sullivan, see [DH1], [DH2], [MSS]. For an introduction to complex iteration the review paper by P. Blanchard [Bl] is recommended. For an introduction to the Mandelbrot set the beautiful book by H.-O. Peitgen and P. Richter [PR] is recommended and therein the paper by A. Douady [D2].

This paper reviews part of what is known about the Mandelbrot set. We will give proofs only when the argument is simple. The proofs for most statements in the paper are much more involved and require a solid background in complex analysis. Sometimes an idea of a proof is mentioned. The reader is not assumed to be able to fill the gaps, but is encouraged to dig into the references.

I thank Adrien Douady and John H. Hubbard for inspiration, explanations and discussions over the years, Homer Smith for providing the Colored Plates 1–12, Yuval Fisher for providing most of the computer pictures in the paper and the Max Planck Institut für Mathematik for hospitality when writing this paper.

2. The dynamical plane. Any complex quadratic polynomial P can be conjugated to a *unique* polynomial of the form

$$P_c(z) = z^2 + c$$

by an affine change of the z-variable, which allows a change of the origin and a change of the scale; i.e. there exists a map $h(z) = az + b$ such that $h^{-1} \circ P \circ h = P_c$. In order to understand all quadratic polynomials under iteration it is sufficient to understand the one-parameter family $\{P_c\}_{c \in \mathbf{C}}$. The polynomial P_c has a unique *critical point*: $\omega = 0$, i.e. a point ω where the

derivative $P'(\omega)$ equals 0. The parameter value c is called the *critical value*:
$c = P_c(0)$.

Since both the variable z and the parameter c fill out a plane, it can cause
some confusion; in particular because we shall jump back and forth between
these planes. For a fixed c we refer to the z-plane as *the dynamical plane
for P_c*, while we refer to the c-plane as *the parameter plane*.

It is important to realize that *every* point in the parameter plane gives rise
to its own special picture in the dynamical plane.

For a polynomial P the sequence

$$z_0, z_1 = P(z_0), \ldots, z_{n+1} = P(z_n), \ldots$$

is called the *orbit* of z_0 under iteration. A point z_0 is called *preperiodic* if

$$z_{k+l} = z_l \quad \text{for some } k \geq 1 \text{ and } l \geq 0,$$

periodic of period k if

$$z_k = z_0 \quad \text{and} \quad z_j \neq z_0 \quad \text{for } 0 < j < k$$

and *strictly periodic* if $l > 0$. In the periodic case the orbit of z_0 is called a
cycle.

For a periodic point z_0 of period k define the *multiplier* (or *eigenvalue*)
ρ of the cycle as the derivative of $P^{\circ k}$ at z_0; using the chain rule we see that

$$\rho = (P^{\circ k})'(z_0) = \prod_{j=0}^{k-1} P'(z_j),$$

so that the derivative of $P^{\circ k}$ is the same at all points of the cycle.

We call a cycle

(i)	*attracting*	if $|\rho| < 1$,
(ii)	*superattracting*	if $\rho = 0$,
(iii)	*repelling*	if $|\rho| > 1$,
(iv)	*indifferent* (or *neutral*)	if $|\rho| = 1$.

Note that a cycle is superattracting if and only if a critical point belongs to
the cycle.

The Taylor series of $P^{\circ k}$ at a periodic point z_0 of multiplier ρ begins

$$P^{\circ k}(z_0 + u) = z_0 + \rho u + \cdots,$$

so if $|\rho| < 1$ and z is sufficiently close to z_0 then the iterate $P^{\circ k}(z)$ is closer to
z_0 than z, $P^{\circ 2k}(z)$ even closer etc. This explains the name: attracting cycle.
If $|\rho| > 1$ and z is sufficiently close to z_0 then the iterate $P^{\circ k}(z)$ is further
away from z_0 than z. This explains the name: repelling cycle.

EXAMPLE 1. The fixed points for P_c are the solutions to the equation
$z^2 + c = z$:

$$z = (1 \pm \sqrt{1 - 4c})/2$$

with multiplier

(1) $$\rho = 1 \pm \sqrt{1 - 4c}.$$

For $c \neq 1/4$ there are two fixed points, which are symmetrical around $1/2$. We denote the fixed points by α_c and β_c where β_c is the name of the most repelling fixed point (this is meaningful whenever the two fixed points are not symmetrical around the real axis).

The periodic points of period 2 are the solutions to the equation $(z^2 + c)^2 + c = z$ which are not fixed points:

$$z = (-1 \pm \sqrt{-3 - 4c})/2$$

with multiplier

(2) $$\rho = 4(1 + c).$$

For $c \neq -3/4$ there are two points of period 2 forming one cycle.

Each polynomial has infinitely many cycles: attracting, repelling or indifferent. In 1905 P. Fatou proved the following very surprising result:

THEOREM 1 (P. FATOU). *Every attracting cycle for a polynomial (or a rational function) attracts at least one critical point.*

A proof can be found in [D1] or in [Br].

A polynomial of degree $d \geq 2$ can therefore have at most $d - 1$ attracting cycles in the plane. In particular a quadratic polynomial P_c can have at most one attracting cycle.

This is the first result to support the statement:

the dynamical behaviour is dominated by

the behaviour of the critical points.

The dynamical plane for P decomposes into two disjoint subsets: the set of seeds with bounded orbit and the set of seeds with unbounded orbit. We denote by K_P the set of seeds with *bounded* orbit:

$$K_P = \{z \in \mathbf{C} | P^{\circ n}(z) \nrightarrow \infty\}.$$

All the cycles are of course contained in K_P. We denote by $A_P(\infty)$ the set of seeds with *unbounded* orbit:

$$A_P(\infty) = \mathbf{C} - K_P = \{z \in \mathbf{C} | P^{\circ n}(z) \rightarrow \infty\}.$$

The dynamical plane for P can also be decomposed into two other disjoint subsets: the *stable* set on which the dynamics are tame and the *Julia set* J_P on which the dynamics are chaotic. The set $A_P(\infty)$ is called the *attractive basin* of ∞. It is completely invariant under iteration, i.e. invariant under both forward and backward iteration. The set K_P is called the *filled-in Julia set*, since $\partial K_P = \partial A_P(\infty) = J_P$. The reader is referred to [Bl] or [K] for a more detailed discussion of Julia sets. But for completeness we mention that all the repelling cycles are contained in J_P and that all the preimages of any point $z_0 \in J_P$ form a dense set of J_P; in fact

$$J_P = \text{closure}\{\text{repelling cycles}\}$$

$$= \text{closure} \left(\bigcup_{n \geq 0} P^{-n}(z_0) \right) \quad \text{for any } z_0 \in J_P.$$

The last property with $z_0 = \beta_c$ was used to produce the computer drawings of the Julia sets shown in this paper.

REMARK 1. It is only when dealing with a polynomial P that we can define the Julia set J_P without referring to *normal families* of mappings. The definition of the Julia set as the boundary of the filled-in Julia set relies on the fact that the boundary of any completely invariant component (here $A_P(\infty)$) of the complement of the Julia set equals the Julia set.

In 1918-1919 P. Fatou [F] and G. Julia [J] proved another result which further supports the importance of the behaviour of the critical points.

THEOREM 2 (P. FATOU AND G. JULIA). *Let Ω_P denote the set of critical points for a polynomial P. Then*

$$\Omega_P \subset K_P \qquad \Leftrightarrow \qquad J_P \text{ is connected}$$
$$\Omega_P \cap K_P = \emptyset \qquad \Rightarrow \qquad J_P \text{ is a Cantor set.}$$

The theorem treats the two extreme cases where either all the critical points or none of the critical points have bounded orbits.

For a quadratic polynomial there is only one critical point. The Julia set (and the filled-in Julia) set is therefore either connected or a Cantor set.

REMARK 2. a) Any totally disconnected, compact, perfect set is homeomorphic to the Cantor middle-third set and therefore deserves the name *a Cantor set*.

b) For $d > 2$ the Julia set J_P can be a Cantor set even if $\Omega_P \cap K_P \neq \emptyset$. But there are also other possibilities. A complete characterization of the Julia sets of cubic polynomials is contained in [BH2].

Every filled-in Julia set K_P is closed and bounded, i.e. compact.

We shall only estimate the bound of the filled-in Julia set for a quadratic polynomial P_c. Let $R = \max(2, |c|)$. Then the following inequality holds for $|z| > R$:

(3) $$\frac{|P_c(z)|}{|z|} \geq |z| - \frac{|c|}{|z|} \geq |z| - 1 > 1.$$

Hence

$$\text{if } |z| > R \quad \text{then } P_c^{\circ n}(z) \to \infty.$$

In other words K_c is completely contained in the disc centered at the origin and with radius $R = \max(2, |c|)$.

3. The parameter plane. The goal is to decompose the parameter plane into regions corresponding to *qualitatively* different dynamical behaviour.

The dichotomy for the dynamical behaviour expressed by the Julia set J_c being either connected or a Cantor set determines a natural decomposition of the parameter plane. By Theorem 2 this dichotomy is also expressed by the critical point 0 having either a bounded orbit or not under iteration by P_c; a property which is easy to check by computer. The plane is decomposed into the Mandelbrot set

$$M = \{c \in \mathbf{C} | J_c \text{ is connected}\}$$
$$= \{c \in \mathbf{C} | P_c^{on}(0) \nrightarrow \infty\}$$
$$= \{c \in \mathbf{C} | c, c^2 + c, (c^2 + c)^2 + c, \ldots \nrightarrow \infty\}$$

and its complement $\mathbf{C} - M$.

Let us again emphasize the difference between the question we ask in the dynamical plane and in the parameter plane. In the dynamical plane we fix a parameter value c and study orbits under iteration of P_c for all seeds. In the parameter plane we fix the seed $z_0 = 0$ and study the orbit of 0 for all parameter values. The seed $z_0 = 0$ is—as we have seen—not an arbitrary choice, but the unique critical point for each P_c.

The decomposition of the parameter plane into M and its complement $\mathbf{C} - M$ may look very rough. It is not at all clear from the definition why the components of $\mathbf{C} - \partial M$ in fact determine the detailed decomposition of the parameter plane we want and why the boundary ∂M is the bifurcation set, i.e. the set of parameter values for which the dynamical behaviour changes qualitatively. The reason is—as mentioned earlier—that the dynamical behaviour of any P_c is dominated by the behaviour of the critical point 0.

By using inequality (3) in §2 we get:

If $|c| > 2$ then $|P_c^{o2}(0)| > |c|$ and $P_c^{on}(0) \to \infty$.

If $|c| \le 2$ and $|P_c^{ok}(0)| > 2$ for some k, then $P_c^{on}(0) \to \infty$.

Hence if the orbit of 0 under P_c ever gets outside the closed disc centered at the origin with radius 2, then $c \notin M$. Furthermore we conclude that the Mandelbrot set is completely contained in the closed disc centered at the origin with radius 2

$$M \subset \{c \in \mathbf{C} | |c| \le 2\}.$$

The estimate is best possible, since $-2 \in M$. In fact it is easy to show that 0 has a bounded orbit under P_c with c real if and only if $c \in [-2, 1/4]$. Hence

$$M \cap \mathbf{R} = [-2, 1/4].$$

A computer program producing M. (a) Choose an integer N, the maximal number of iterations the computer is asked to do.

(b) Choose a real number $R \ge 2$.

(c) Color c black if $|P_c^{on}(0)| \le R$ for all $n \le N$.

(d) Otherwise color c in color n where n is the smallest number so that $|P_c^{\circ n}(0)| > R$.

An approximation of the Mandelbrot set is then seen in black as shown in Figure 5. This computer drawing is made by using the program Super MANDELZOOM [**Mo**].

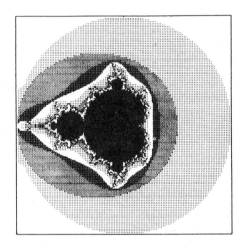

FIGURE 5

The first computer pictures made by Benoit B. Mandelbrot were exclusively in black and white, by setting color n to white for all n. Without some coloring of the complement of the Mandelbrot set as described by (d) in the algorithm above, it is not possible to get a feeling for the finer details, since the filaments often are so thin that they are smaller than the size of a pixel. It is John H. Hubbard's merit to have colored the complement. The idea is closely related to how we understand M as we shall see in §6.

Figures 1–4 showing the boundary of M are drawn by using another algorithm in order to thicken the boundary. This can be done as described by J. Milnor in [**M1**] or as described by Y. Fisher in [**Fi**].

The analysis of the Mandelbrot set in the rest of this paper is divided into the analysis of the interior (this section), the exterior (§6) and the boundary (§9).

Hyperbolic components of the Mandelbrot set. From Theorem 1 it is clear that any c-value for which there exists an attracting cycle is contained in M. Let $H(M)$ denote the set of such c-values

$$H(M) = \{c \in \mathbf{C} \,|\, P_c \text{ has an attracting cycle}\}.$$

Recall that the attracting cycle is unique.

Applying the implicit function theorem it follows that $H(M)$ is an open set and that there is assigned an invariant to each connected component: the period of the attracting cycle. A connected component W of $H(M)$ is called a *hyperbolic component* of M. (The set of c-values for which the polynomial P_c is hyperbolic is $H(M) \cup (\mathbf{C} - M)$.) It is not known if $H(M)$ equals the interior of M. This open problem goes under the name:

The hyperbolicity conjecture for polynomials in degree 2:

$$\text{int}(M) = H(M).$$

EXAMPLE 2. It is easy to determine the subsets of M for which P_c has an attracting fixed point or an attracting cycle of period 2. We set

(4) $W_0 = \{c \in \mathbf{C} | P_c \text{ has an attracting fixed point}\}$,

(5) $W_{1/2} = \{c \in \mathbf{C} | P_c \text{ has an attracting cycle of period 2}\}$.

The parametrization P_c of quadratic polynomials is convenient when we focus on the behaviour of the critical point. If we focus on the behaviour of a fixed point with a given multiplier the following parametrization is convenient:

$$Q_\lambda(z) = \lambda z + z^2.$$

A polynomial Q_λ has a fixed point at 0 with multiplier $Q'_\lambda(0) = \lambda$. Hence 0 is an attracting fixed point for Q_λ if and only if $|\lambda| < 1$. The polynomial Q_λ is affine conjugated to the polynomial P_c with

$$c = \lambda/2 - (\lambda/2)^2.$$

The unit circle $\lambda = e^{2\pi i t}$ in the λ-plane corresponds to a cardioid in the c-plane parametrized by

(6) $\gamma_{W_0}(t) = e^{2\pi i t}/2 - (e^{2\pi i t}/2)^2.$

This is the big cardioid seen in Figure 1. Therefore W_0 is the subset of M bounded by this cardioid. The subset W_0 is an example of a hyperbolic component.

Whenever we parametrize the unit circle we shall use the form $e^{2\pi i t}$, $t \in \mathbf{T} = \mathbf{R}/\mathbf{Z}$, where the unit for arguments is one turn.

The multiplier of the attracting fixed point α_c for P_c with $c \in W_0$ defines the following map into the unit disc D:

(7) $$\rho_{W_0}: W_0 \to D$$
$$c \mapsto 1 - \sqrt{1 - 4c}$$

where $\sqrt{\ }$ denotes the principal branch of the square root. The inverse map $\lambda \mapsto c$ is given above. Notice that $\rho_{W_0}: W_0 \to D$ is a conformal isomorphism which extends continuously to the boundary. The boundary point $\gamma_{W_0}(t)$ is said to have *internal argument* t.

Using (2) we find immediately that $W_{1/2}$ is the open disc centered at $c = -1$ with radius $1/4$. The subset $W_{1/2}$ is also an example of a hyperbolic component. The multiplier of the attracting cycle of period 2 for P_c with $c \in W_{1/2}$ defines the following map into the unit disc:

(8)
$$\rho_{W_{1/2}} \colon W_{1/2} \to D$$
$$c \mapsto 4(1 + c).$$

Notice that $\rho_{W_{1/2}} \colon W_{1/2} \to D$ is a conformal isomorphism which extends continuously to the boundary.

The closure of the two sets has one point in common:
$$\overline{W}_0 \cap \overline{W}_{1/2} = \{-3/4\}.$$

The point $c = -3/4$ is the *period doubling bifurcation* point: when c changes from being inside the big cardioid to inside the disc, then α_c changes from being attracting to repelling, and the cycle of period 2 changes from being repelling to attracting.

One can show that for each $p/q \in \mathbf{Q}/\mathbf{Z} - \{0\}$ there is a hyperbolic component $W_{p/q}$ satisfying
$$\overline{W}_{p/q} \cap \overline{W}_0 = \gamma_{W_0}(p/q).$$

The point $c = \gamma_{W_0}(p/q)$ is a *period q-doubling bifurcation* point: when c changes from being inside the big cardioid to inside the hyperbolic component $W_{p/q}$, then α_c changes from being attracting to repelling, and a cycle of period q changes from being repelling to attracting.

Set

$M^*_{p/q}$ = the connected component of $M - \overline{W}_0$ containing $W_{p/q}$.

The *limb* $M_{p/q}$ of M of interval argument p/q is defined as
$$M_{p/q} = M^*_{p/q} \cup \gamma_{W_0}(p/q).$$

One can prove that
$$M = \overline{W}_0 \cup \bigcup_{p/q} M_{p/q}$$

([Y] and [L3]), see Figure 6. See also Color Plates 7, 8, and 9, which show the limbs $M_{1/5}$, $M_{2/5}$ and $M_{1/12}$ respectively.

It is easy to see that every hyperbolic component W is simply connected. Let k denote the period of the attracting cycle of any polynomial in W. For any $c \in \mathbf{C}$ set
$$f_n(c) = P_c^{\circ nk}(0).$$

On W the functions f_n converge to a function f such that $f(c)$ is one of the points in the attracting cycle. The convergence is uniformly exponential on any compact subset A of W, i.e. there exist constants $C_A > 0$ and $r_A < 1$ such that
$$|f_n(c) - f(c)| \le C_A r_A^n \quad \text{for all } c \in A.$$

Let γ be a simple closed curve contained in W and let Δ be the closed disc in $\mathbf{C}$ bounded by γ. For each $p > n$ we have
$$|f_P(c) - f_n(c)| \le 2C_\Delta r_\Delta^n \quad \text{for all } c \in \gamma$$

and by the maximum principle then for all $c \in \Delta$. It follows that f_n converges uniformly on Δ to f with $f(c)$ an attracting periodic point with multiplier $\leq r_\Delta$. So Δ is contained in $H(M)$ and hence in W.

Since each hyperbolic component is simply connected it follows from the Riemann mapping theorem that it can be mapped conformally onto the unit disc. In Example 2 we found for the hyperbolic components W_0 and $W_{1/2}$ that the multiplier of the unique attracting cycle explicitly defines such a map. This is true in general.

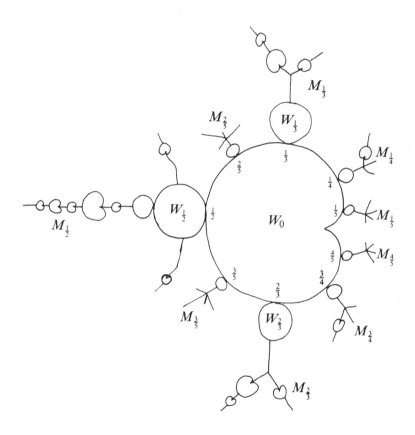

FIGURE 6

THEOREM 3 (A. DOUADY, J. H. HUBBARD AND D. SULLIVAN). *For each hyperbolic component W of M the multiplier ρ_W induces a conformal isomorphism*

$$\rho_W : W \to D$$

which extends to a homeomorphism of $\overline{W}$ onto $\overline{D}$.

There exist several proofs of this result ([**D1**] and [**DH2**]). One proof goes as follows:

1. The mapping $\rho_W\colon W - \{c \text{ superattractive}\} \to D - \{0\}$ is an analytic covering map.

2. The mapping ρ_W is proper, i.e. for any compact subset $K \subset D$ the preimage $\rho_W^{-1}(K)$ is compact as well.

3. The degree of ρ_W is 1.

REMARK 3. Any proper, branched covering has a finite degree (which is constant on every connected component of the domain) and the degree is the number of preimages, counted with multiplicity, of any point in the range. Hence the degree can be determined by the number of preimages of one point. This kind of argumentation is central in complex iteration theory.

Theorem 3 implies that each hyperbolic component has a unique c-value for which the attracting cycle is superattracting. We denote by c_W the *center* of W defined by

$$c_W = \rho_W^{-1}(0).$$

For W_0 and $W_{1/2}$ the centers are $c_{W_0} = 0$ and $c_{W_{1/2}} = -1$. The boundary point

$$\gamma_W(t) = \rho_W^{-1}(e^{2\pi it})$$

is said to have *internal argument* t. The boundary point of internal argument 0 is called the *root* of W. For W_0 and $W_{1/2}$ the roots are $\gamma_{W_0}(0) = 1/4$ and $\gamma_{W_{1/2}}(0) = -3/4$.

The number $\nu(n)$ of hyperbolic components of a given period n equals the number of c-values for which there is a superattracting cycle of period n.

period n	c_W a root of ...	$\nu(n)$
1	$c = 0$	1
2	$c^2 + c = 0$	1
3	$(c^2 + c)^2 + c = 0$	3
4	$[(c^2 + c)^2 + c]^2 + c = 0$	6
5	$[[(c^2 + c)^2 + c]^2 + c]^2 + c = 0$	15

The roots of the polynomials in c are all simple (A. Gleason). The distribution of the hyperbolic components of period 1–5 is shown in Figure 7.

REMARK 4. There is only one type of hyperbolic component for quadratic polynomials—they are all conformally isomorphic to the disc D. For polynomials of higher degree there are several types [M3].

4. **Dynamics of $P_0(z) = z^2$.** The polynomial P_0 is the simplest quadratic polynomial to analyze. As we shall see in the following we can compare the dynamics of any quadratic polynomial with the dynamics of P_0 near ∞.

The filled-in Julia set K_0 equals the closed unit disc $\overline{D}$. The critical point 0 is fixed and superattracting and attracts any point $z_0 \in D$ under iteration. Any point $z_0 \notin \overline{D}$ escapes to ∞ under iteration. The interesting dynamics takes place on the Julia set J_0 which equals the unit circle. The dynamics is determined by doubling the argument:

$$z = e^{2\pi it} \mapsto z^2 = e^{2\pi i 2t}.$$

COLOR PLATE 1

COLOR PLATE 2

COLOR PLATE 3

Color Plates 1, 2, *and* 3 *show successive blow ups of the Mandelbrot set centered around* $c \approx -0.1480798 + i\ 0.6515558$.

COLOR PLATE 4

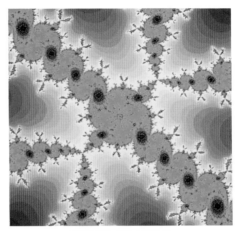

COLOR PLATE 5

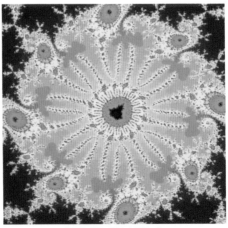

COLOR PLATE 6

Color Plates 4, 5, and 6 show successive blow ups of the Mandelbrot set centered around
$c \approx -0.124422584 + i\, 0.839099345$. *Notice the binary structure of different decorations around the copy of the Mandelbrot set.*

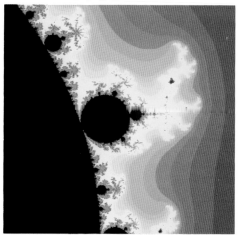

COLOR PLATE 7

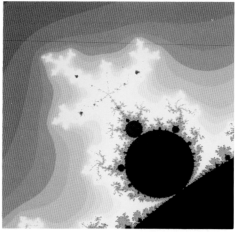

COLOR PLATE 8

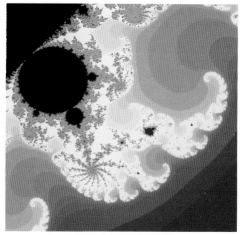

COLOR PLATE 9

Color Plates 7, 8, and 9 show limbs of the Mandelbrot set: the limb $M_{1/5}$, $M_{2/5}$ and $M_{1/12}$ respectively.

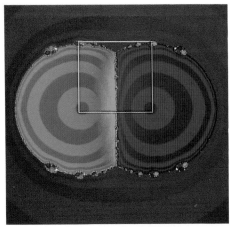

COLOR PLATE 10

COLOR PLATE 11

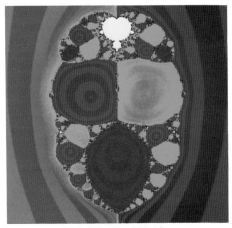

COLOR PLATE 12

Color Plates 10, 11, and 12 show successive blow ups in the λ-parameter plane for Newton's method applied to cubic polynomials of the form P_λ. The center of the yellow copy of the Mandelbrot set is $\lambda \approx i\ 0.333$.

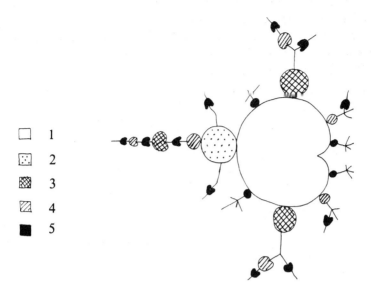

☐	1
⬚	2
▨	3
▨	4
■	5

FIGURE 7

The points $t \in \mathbf{T} = \mathbf{R}/\mathbf{Z}$ which are preperiodic under doubling are the rational numbers. The rationals with odd denominator are all periodic and the rationals with even denominator are all strictly preperiodic. This follows from the fact that

$$t = \frac{n}{2^k - 1} \quad \text{for some } k \geq 1, n \geq 1$$

is periodic of period k or a divisor of k, and that each rational number with odd denominator can be written in this form for some n and k. For instance $1/5 = 3/15$.

period	cycles
1	$0 \mapsto 0$
2	$1/3 \mapsto 2/3 \mapsto 1/3$
3	$1/7 \mapsto 2/7 \mapsto 4/7 \mapsto 1/7;$
	$3/7 \mapsto 6/7 \mapsto 5/7 \mapsto 3/7$
4	$1/15 \mapsto 2/15 \mapsto 4/15 \mapsto 8/15 \mapsto 1/15;$
	$3/15 \mapsto 6/15 \mapsto 12/15 \mapsto 9/15 \mapsto 3/15;$
	$7/15 \mapsto 14/15 \mapsto 13/15 \mapsto 11/15 \mapsto 7/15.$

5. The main tools for understanding the dynamics. For any compact set K in the plane there exists a Green's function $G(K): \mathbf{C} - K \to \mathbf{R}$ defined on the complement. It is a harmonic function which has a logarithmic pole at ∞ and tends to 0 towards K. By these properties $G(K)$ is uniquely determined. In general it is difficult to define explicitly the Green's function for a compact set K. It is therefore quite surprising that if K is either the filled-in Julia set for a polynomial or the Mandelbrot set, then it is rather easy to define the Green's function using the dynamics.

The main tools for understanding the dynamics of a quadratic polynomial P_c under iteration are the Green's function G_c and the φ_c-map to be defined below. Both mappings are defined dynamically.

The Green's function G_c of a filled-in Julia set K_c. We define the function $G_c : \mathbf{C} - K_c \to \mathbf{R}$ by

$$G_c(z) = \lim_{n \to \infty} 2^{-n} \log(|P_c^{\circ n}(z)|).$$

One can prove ([**DH2**]) that
  (1) G_c is harmonic,
  (2) $G_c(P_c(z)) = 2G_c(z)$,
  (3) $G_c(z) = \log|z| + O(1)$ when $|z| \to \infty$,
  (4) $G_c(z) \to 0$ when $d(z, K_c) \to 0$.

Hence G_c is the Green's function for the filled-in Julia set K_c. The mapping G_c measures the escape rate to ∞. We can extend the map G_c to a continuous map on $\mathbf{C}$ by defining $G_c(K_c) = 0$.

The φ_c-map for a polynomial P_c. If we extend the complex plane to the Riemann sphere $\bar{\mathbf{C}} = \mathbf{C} \cup \{\infty\}$ by adding ∞ and extend the polynomial by $P_c(\infty) = \infty$, then the point at ∞ is a superattracting fixed point. From this observation it follows that there exists an analytic isomorphism φ_c defined in a neighborhood $(\mathbf{C}, \infty)$ of ∞, conjugating P_c to the simplest quadratic polynomial $P_0(z) = z^2$, i.e. the following diagram commutes:

$$
\begin{array}{ccc}
(\mathbf{C}, \infty) & \xrightarrow{\ P_c\ } & (\mathbf{C}, \infty) \\
\varphi_c \downarrow & & \downarrow \varphi_c \\
(\mathbf{C}, \infty) & \xrightarrow[\ P_0\ ]{} & (\mathbf{C}, \infty)
\end{array}
$$

The φ_c-map can be defined near ∞ by

$$\varphi_c(z) = \lim_{n \to \infty} (P_c^{\circ n}(z))^{1/2^n}.$$

This expression is not well defined though unless we specify the choice of the root. For each n we can formally rewrite $(P_c^{\circ n}(z))^{1/2^n}$ as follows:

$$(P_c^{\circ n}(z))^{1/2^n} = z \frac{(P_c(z))^{1/2}}{z} \frac{(P_c^{\circ 2}(z))^{1/4}}{(P_c(z))^{1/2}} \cdots \frac{(P_c^{\circ n}(z))^{1/2^n}}{(P_c^{\circ(n-1)}(z))^{1/2^{(n-1)}}}$$

and the $(k-1)$st quotient can be rewritten as

$$(1 + c/(P_c^{\circ k}(z))^2)^{1/2^{(k+1)}}.$$

For z sufficiently big we have $|P_c^{\circ k}(z)|^2 > |c|$ for all k. Hence we can choose the 2^{k+1}-root to be the principal root. The correct definition of φ_c is therefore

$$\varphi_c(z) = z \prod_{n=0}^{\infty} (1 + c/(P_c^{\circ k}(z))^2)^{1/2^{(k+1)}}$$

with the principal roots chosen.

One can prove [**DH2**] that φ_c can be extended in a unique way to $U_c = \{z | G_c(z) > G_c(0)\}$ so that

$$\varphi_c \colon U_c \to \mathbf{C} - \overline{D}_{\exp(G_c(0))}$$

is an analytic isomorphism conjugating P_c to P_0:

$$\psi_c(P_c(\cdot)) = (\varphi_c(\cdot))^2.$$

The map φ_c is the only analytic isomorphism conjugating P_c to P_0 and $\varphi_c(z)$ defines therefore canonical coordinates on U_c.

One can furthermore prove that the map $\varphi_c(z)$ is analytic in both z and c.

The connection between G_c and φ_c is given by

$$G_c(z) = \log|\varphi_c(z)| \quad \text{for } z \in U_c.$$

Suppose $P_0^{\circ n}(0) \nrightarrow \infty$. If $P_c^{\circ n}(0) \nrightarrow \infty$ then $U_c = \mathbf{C} - K_c$ and $\varphi_c \colon \mathbf{C} - K_c \to \mathbf{C} - \overline{D}$ is a conformal representation of the complement of the filled-in Julia set.

For each $r > 1$ the *equipotential* $\Gamma_c(r)$ defined by

$$\Gamma_c(r) = G_c^{-1}(\log r) = \varphi_c^{-1}(\{re^{2\pi i\theta}\}_{0\leq\theta\leq 1})$$

is a simple closed curve surrounding the filled-in Julia set K_c (see Figure 8).

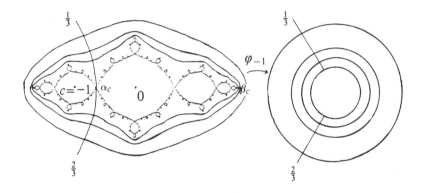

FIGURE 8

This proves in fact (part of Theorem 2) that the filled-in Julia set is connected, since

$$K_c = \bigcap_{r>1} V_c(r)$$

where $V_c(r)$ is the closed, simply connected domain bounded by $\Gamma_c(r)$. The orthogonal trajectories of the equipotentials are called *external rays*. A ray of *external argument* θ is defined by

$$R_c(\theta) = \varphi_c^{-1}(\{re^{2\pi i\theta}\}_{1<r<\infty})$$

(see Figures 8 and 11–15). We shall come back to the importance of the rays in §8, and in particular the importance of the rays with rational arguments.

Suppose $P_c^{\circ n}(0) \to \infty$. If $P_c^{\circ n}(0) \to \infty$ then $G_c(0) > 0$ and $G_c(c) = 2G_c(0)$, so $\varphi_c(c)$ is defined. This property is essential for the definition of the map ϕ_M in the next section.

For each $r > e^{G_c(0)}$ the equipotential $\Gamma_c(r) = G_c^{-1}(\log r)$ is a simple closed curve surrounding the filled-in Julia set as before. But for $r = e^{G_c(0)}$ the equipotential $\Gamma_c(r)$ is a figure eight, see Figure 9.

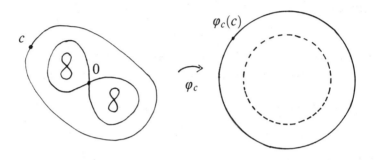

FIGURE 9

Inside each lobe of the figure eight is a preimage of the figure eight, etc. In this way one can prove (the other part of Theorem 2) that the filled-in Julia set is a Cantor set.

6. The main tools for understanding M. The Mandelbrot set is a compact set in the plane, so there exists a unique Green's function $G_M: \mathbf{C} - M \to \mathbf{R}$. In the parameter plane there is no dynamics, but the function is induced by the dynamically defined functions G_c.

Furthermore there exists an analytic map

$$\phi_M : \mathbf{C} - M \to \mathbf{C} - \overline{D}$$

defined by

(9) $$\phi_M(c) = \varphi_c(c)$$

remembering that c belongs to U_c, so that $\varphi_c(c)$ is always defined. The mapping ϕ_M relates the dynamical planes to the parameter plane.

THEOREM 4 (A. DOUADY AND J. H. HUBBARD). *The mapping*

$$\phi_M : \mathbf{C} - M \to \mathbf{C} - \overline{D}$$

defined in (9) *is a conformal isomorphism.*

We shall not give the proof (see [**DH2**]), but only point out that the idea is the following:

1. The mapping ϕ_M is analytic.

2. The mapping ϕ_M is proper, i.e. for every compact set in $\mathbf{C} - \overline{D}$ the inverse image is compact as well.

3. The degree of ϕ_M is 1.

From the conformal representation $\phi_M: \mathbf{C} - M \rightarrow \mathbf{C} - \overline{D}$ we immediately get the harmonic function

$$G_M(c) = \log|\phi_M(c)| = G_c(c).$$

For each $r > 1$ the *equipotential* $\Gamma_M(r)$ defined by

$$\Gamma_M(r) = G_M^{-1}(\log r) = \phi_M^{-1}(\{re^{2\pi i\theta}\}_{0 \le \theta \le 1})$$

is a simple closed curve surrounding the Mandelbrot set (see Figure 5 and Figure 10). An equipotential curve consists of values of c for which 0 escapes to ∞ at a fixed rate.

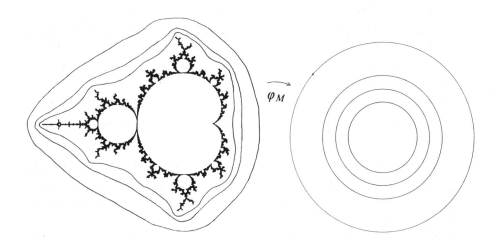

FIGURE 10

REMARK 5. The curves between different colors in Figure 5 are approximations to the equipotential curves. The approximations become more accurate the bigger we choose the radius R. (In Figure 5 the radius was chosen to be 2.)

Moreover Theorem 4 implies

COROLLARY 5 (A. DOUADY AND J. H. HUBBARD). *The Mandelbrot set is connected.*

The proof is similar to the proof of the statement that the filled-in Julia set K_c is connected if $P_c^{\circ n}(0) \nrightarrow \infty$. Let $V_M(r)$ denote the closed, simply connected domain bounded by $\Gamma_M(r)$. Then

$$M = \bigcap_{r>1} V_M(r).$$

Hence M is connected. A set which equals the intersection of a nested sequence of sets homeomorphic to solid balls is called *cellular*. Corollary 5 could therefore have been stated as: The Mandelbrot set is cellular, in particular connected.

Applying the maximum principle we conclude that the Mandelbrot set is simply connected.

It is not known whether M is arcwise connected, but it is proved in [**BD**], using surgery technique, that the principal vein in the limb $M_{1/3}$ is a topological arc. The same technique can be applied to several other cases.

The orthogonal trajectories of the equipotentials are called *external rays* of M. A ray of *external argument* θ is defined by

$$R_M(\theta) = \phi_M^{-1}(\{re^{2\pi i\theta}\}_{1<r<\infty})$$

(see Figure 19). The rays with rational arguments play a special role.

In order to understand why the conformal representation of the complement of M gives so much information about M, we need to discuss further the information we get from the conformal representation φ_c in the dynamical planes for special choices of c.

REMARK 6. The set $C(d)$ analogous to M for polynomials of degree $d > 2$ is also cellular. This is proved in degree 3 in [**BH1**] and for all $d > 3$ by P. Lavaurs.

7. Dynamics of special quadratic polynomials. We have described centers and roots of hyperbolic components. There is a third type of parameter value which plays an important role when dissecting the Mandelbrot set: the Misiurewicz points.

A point c is called a *Misiurewicz point* if the orbit of 0 under P_c is strictly preperiodic. Two easy examples of Misiurewicz points are $c = i$ and $c = -2$:

$$P_i: 0 \mapsto i \mapsto -1 + i \mapsto -i \mapsto -1 + i;$$
$$P_{-2}: 0 \mapsto -2 \mapsto 2 \mapsto 2.$$

For $c = -2$ the filled-in Julia set is the interval on the real axis $[-2, 2]$ which therefore equals the Julia set.

One can prove for any Misiurewicz point c that

$$(10) \qquad\qquad\qquad J_c = K_c.$$

Hence c belongs to J_c. This property is essential. A connected Julia set is called a *dendrite* when (10) is satisfied.

Figure 14 shows the Julia set for the Misiurewicz point $c = i$ and Figure 15 shows the Julia set for $c \approx -0.101096 + i0.956287$ another Misiurewicz point.

The centers and the Misiurewicz points form precisely the set of c-values for which the orbit of 0 under P_c is finite. As we have seen the centers are contained in the interior of M, while the Misiurewicz points are on the boundary of M, since there exist arbitrarily small perturbations of P_c such that 0 escapes to ∞.

One can prove that if c either belongs to a hyperbolic component or if c is a Misiurewicz point, then the filled-in Julia set is locally connected, i.e. for every $z \in K_c$ and for every neighborhood $U \subset K_c$ of z, there exists a connected neighborhood $V \subset U$ in K_c of z.

If K_c is locally connected, then it follows from a theorem by Carathéodory that the conformal representation

$$\psi_c = \varphi_c^{-1} : \mathbf{C} - \overline{D} \to \mathbf{C} - K_c$$

has a continuous extension to the boundary:

$$\gamma_c : \mathbf{T} = \mathbf{R}/\mathbf{Z} \to J_c$$
$$t \mapsto \psi_c(e^{2\pi i t}).$$

Hence if K_c is locally connected then every external ray $R_c(\theta)$ lands at a point $\gamma_c(\theta)$ on the Julia set and γ_c is a parametrization of J_c. A point on the Julia set may be the end point for several rays.

It follows that

$$P_c(R_c(t)) = R_c(2t) \quad \text{and} \quad P_c(\gamma_c(t)) = \gamma_c(2t).$$

Suppose c is a center of a hyperbolic component of period k. Then the critical value c is in the interior of K_c, and c is a superattracting fixed point for $P_c^{\circ k}$. Let U_1 denote the component of $K_c - J_c$ containing c. Then there exists a conjugating map $h_c : \overline{U}_1 \to \overline{D}$, conformal in the interior and continuous on the closure, conjugating $P_c^{\circ k}$ to the polynomial $P_0(z) = z^2$; i.e. the following diagram commutes:

$$
\begin{array}{ccc}
\overline{U}_1 & \xrightarrow{P_c^{\circ k}} & \overline{U}_1 \\
h_c \downarrow & & \downarrow h_c \\
\overline{D} & \xrightarrow{P_0} & \overline{D}
\end{array}
$$

There is a unique point

(11) $$y_1 \in \partial U_1 \quad \text{so that } P_c^{\circ k}(y_1) = y_1.$$

The point y_1 is called the *root* of U_1. It is periodic under iteration of P_c with period k or a divisor of k. The point y_1 belongs to J_c and determines some arguments $\gamma_c^{-1}(y_1)$ which are periodic with period k under doubling. There are always two rays consecutive to U_1 and landing at y_1. (We get two rays for $c = 0$ if we count the real axis twice: with arguments 0 and 1.)

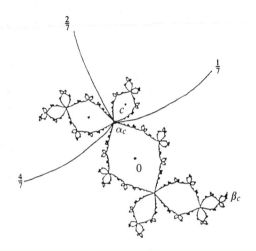

FIGURE 11

To give an idea of the general picture when c is a center of a hyperbolic component we shall give four examples.

EXAMPLE 3. Figure 8 shows the Julia set for $c = -1$ where 0 is periodic of period 2. The root point y_1 is the fixed point α_c. There are two rays landing at y_1: the arguments are $1/3$ and $2/3$.

Figure 11 shows the Julia set for $c \approx -0.12256 + i0.74486$ where 0 is periodic of period 3. The Julia set is called the Douady Rabbit. The root point y_1 is again the fixed point α_c. There are three rays landing at y_1: the arguments are $1/7$, $2/7$ and $4/7$. Notice that the two rays consecutive to U_1 are of argument $1/7$ and $2/7$.

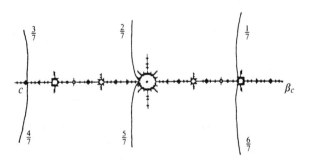

FIGURE 12

Figure 12 shows the Julia set for $c \approx -1.75488$ where 0 is again periodic of period 3, but this time real. The root point y_1 is of period 3. There are two rays landing at y_1: the arguments are 3/7 and 4/7.

Figure 13 shows the Julia set for $c \approx -0.15652 + i1.03225$ where 0 is periodic of period 4. The root point y_1 is of period 4. There are two rays landing at y_1: the arguments are 3/15 and 1/15.

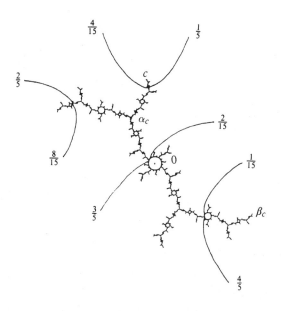

FIGURE 13

Suppose c is a Misiurewicz point. The point c is contained in the dendrite $J_c = K_c$ and determines some arguments $\gamma_c^{-1}(c)$ which are strictly preperiodic under doubling. To give an idea of the general picture when c is a Misiurewicz point we shall give two examples.

EXAMPLE 4. Figure 14 shows the Julia set for $c = i$. The point $c = i$ is the end point for the external ray of argument 1/6.

Figure 15 shows the Julia set for $c \approx -0.101096 + i0.956287$ where the orbit of 0 is as follows:

$$x_0 = 0 \mapsto x_1 = c \mapsto x_2 \mapsto x_3 \mapsto x_4 \mapsto x_5 = x_4.$$

The fixed point $\alpha_c = x_4 = x_5$ is the end point for the external rays of arguments 1/7, 2/7 and 4/7. The point c is the end point for the external rays of arguments 9/56, 11/56 and 15/56.

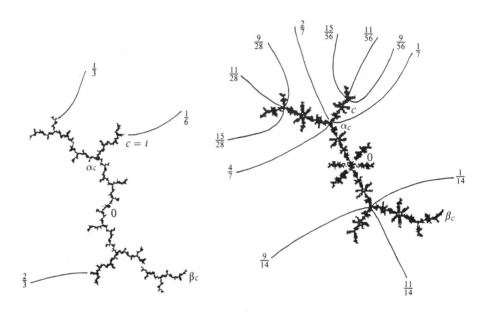

FIGURE 14   FIGURE 15

8. Rational rays of the Mandelbrot set. It would be very desirable to know whether the Mandelbrot set is locally connected or not. If locally connected then we could conclude from the theorem by Carathéodory, that the conformal map $\phi_M^{-1} : \mathbf{C} - \overline{D} \to \mathbf{C} - M$ could be extended continuously to the boundary. We would get a parametrization of ∂M and we would know that all the external rays land on ∂M. Every computer picture supports the following conjecture, but nobody has been able to prove it.

Main conjecture: M is locally connected.

One can prove that if M is locally connected then the interior of M equals the union of hyperbolic components.

Furthermore it would follow that M is arcwise connected, since a set which is connected and locally connected is also arcwise connected.

In order to show what we are up against we give two examples of a set which is connected but not locally connected. The set to the left in Figure 16 is formed by the box $\{(x,y) | -1 \le x \le 0, -1 \le y \le 1\}$ and a comb. This set is arcwise connected. The set to the right in Figure 16 is formed by the same box as before and the graph of $\sin 1/x$, $0 < x \le 1$. This set is not arcwise connected. In both cases the set is compact so there exists a Green's function on the complement. None of the points on the line segment $\{(0,y) | -1 < y < 1\}$ can be reached from outside following external rays.

REMARK 7. It has been proved that the set $C(d)$ analogous to M for polynomials of degree $d > 2$ is not locally connected (see [M2] and [L2]).

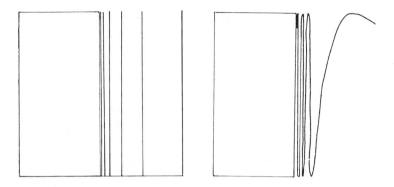

FIGURE 16

FIGURE 17

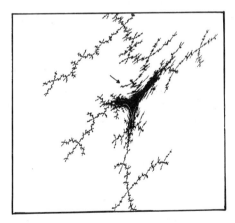

FIGURE 18

Two details of the real part of $C(3)$ are shown in Figures 17 and 18. The computer drawings are made by J. Milnor. Notice the resemblance between these drawings and the examples shown in Figure 16 respectively.

Although we do not know whether M is locally connected or not it is surprisingly enough possible to prove that every external ray with rational argument $t = p/q$ lands. We shall call the end point $\gamma_M(t)$.

THEOREM 6 (A. DOUADY AND J. H. HUBBARD). (1) *For every rational argument $t = p/q$ the external ray $R_M(t)$ lands at a point $c = \gamma_M(t)$ which is either a root of a hyperbolic component or a Misiurewicz point.*

(2) *If t is periodic of period k under doubling then c is the root of a hyperbolic component W of period k. Let c_W denote the center of W. In the dynamical plane for P_{c_W} let y_1 denote the root of the component U_1 of $K_{c_W} - J_{c_W}$ containing c_W and let $\{t_1, t_2\} \subset \gamma_{c_W}^{-1}(y_1)$ be the arguments of the two external rays consecutive to U_1 and landing at y_1. Then $\gamma_M^{-1}(c) = \{t_1, t_2\}$.*

(3) *If t is strictly preperiodic under doubling then $c = \gamma_M(t)$ is a Misiurewicz point, and $\gamma_c^{-1}(c) = \gamma_M^{-1}(c)$.*

The proof is not easy. It is found in [DH2].

To illustrate the theorem we draw the consequences of Examples 3 and 4:

EXAMPLE 5.

$\gamma_M(1/3) = \gamma_M(2/3) = -3/4 =$ the root of $W_{1/2}$;

$\gamma_M(1/7) = \gamma_M(2/7) =$ the root of $W_{1/3}$;

$\gamma_M(3/7) = \gamma_M(4/7) =$ the root of the hyperbolic component of period 3 with center $c_W \approx -1.75488$;

$\gamma_M(3/15) = \gamma_M(4/15) =$ the root of the hyperbolic component of period 4 with center $c_W \approx -0.15652 + i1.03225$;

$\gamma_M(1/6) = i$;

$\gamma_M(9/56) = \gamma_M(11/56) = \gamma_M(15/56) = c \approx -0.101096 + i0.956287$.

We define the following equivalence relation among the rationals in $]0, 1[$:

$$t_1 \sim t_2 \Leftrightarrow \gamma_M(t_1) = \gamma_M(t_2).$$

In particular this equivalence relation defines a pairing of rationals with odd denominator. From the few examples mentioned above one could get the wrong impression that it is easy to find the partner equivalent to a given rational t with odd denominator. This is not the case. But P. Lavaurs [L1] has given an algorithm which recursively determines these equivalence classes.

Lavaurs algorithm. We represent a $t \in]0, 1[$ as the point $e^{2\pi i t}$ on the unit circle S^1. If two rationals with odd denominator are equivalent, then we connect the two corresponding points in S^1 by an arc of a circle in $\overline{D}$ perpendicular to the boundary S^1. Recursively, using the period k of the rationals, we can construct the equivalence classes as follows:

1. Connect $1/3$ and $2/3$.

2. Suppose all points corresponding to rationals of period l for $2 \le l < k$ have been connected. Then points corresponding to rationals of period k are connected pairwise following the two rules:

(i) all arcs are disjoint,

(ii) if t_1 is the smallest rational in $]0, 1[$ of period k which has not yet been connected, then connect t_1 to the smallest possible $t_2 > t_1$ observing rule (i).

The proof of the algorithm is a detailed analysis of the order of periodic points in Julia sets and the order of hyperbolic components in the Mandelbrot set.

We generate the equivalence between rationals with even denominator by taking the closure of the equivalence relation on rationals with odd denominator.

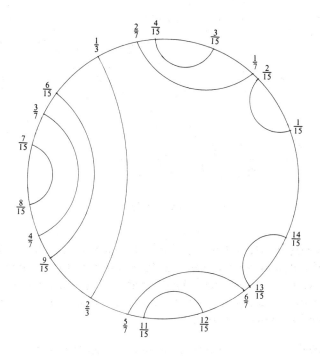

FIGURE 19

Figure 19 shows the arcs drawn for rationals of period k with $2 \le k \le 4$. Figure 20 shows the Mandelbrot set with rational rays of period k with $2 \le k \le 5$.

The abstract Mandelbrot set. From the equivalence relation on rationals we can get a model of an abstract Mandelbrot set as a pinched disc: each connecting arc is pinched to a point. One can prove that the abstract Mandelbrot set is homeomorphic to M if and only if M is locally connected.

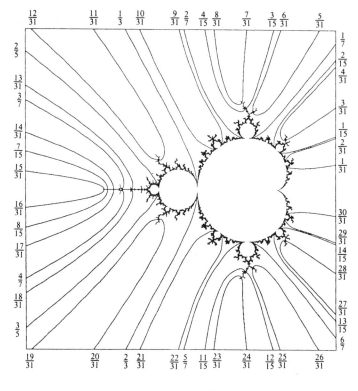

FIGURE 20

9. The boundary of M.

A key tool for P. Fatou and G. Julia in the study of iterations of polynomials and rational functions was the theorem by Montel characterizing normal families. They used it in the description of the dynamics. We shall see how this theorem can be used in the parameter plane to derive the following two results:

1. *The Misiurewicz points are dense in the boundary of M.*

2. *The boundary of M is contained in the closure of the centers of hyperbolic components.*

This gives some justification to why the boundary of M is so complicated.

Normal families of analytic mappings. Let U be an open subset of the Riemann sphere $\bar{C}$ and

$$\mathbf{F} = \{f_n\colon U \to \bar{C}\}$$

a family of analytic mappings. The family $\mathbf{F}$ is a normal family if any subsequence contains a subsequence which converges uniformly on compact subsets of U.

MONTEL'S THEOREM. *Let* **F** *be a family defined on a domain U. If there exist three different points a, b, c in* $\bar{\mathbf{C}}$ *such that*

$$\{a, b, c\} \cap \left(\bigcup_{f \in \mathbf{F}} f(U) \right) = \varnothing$$

then **F** *is a normal family on U.*

We shall consider the family of functions $f_n \colon \mathbf{C} \to \mathbf{C}$ defined recursively as

$$f_1(c) = c; \qquad f_n(c) = (f_{n-1}(c))^2 + c.$$

For a fixed c the sequence $(0, f_1(c), \ldots, f_n(c), \ldots)$ is nothing but the orbit of 0 of the polynomial P_c.

Let c_0 be a boundary point of M. For any $c \in \mathbf{C} - M$ we have $f_n(c) \to \infty$, while for any $c \in M$ we have $|f_n(c)| \leq 2$. Hence for any neighborhood U of c_0 the family $f_n|_U \colon U \to \mathbf{C}$ is not normal.

In order to prove the first statement above we shall assume that it is false. Assume that $c_0 \neq 1/4$. We choose U to be a simply connected neighborhood of c_0 so that $1/4 \notin U$ and so that U contains no Misiurewicz points for which 0 is eventually mapped onto a fixed point. Let $g_1, g_2 \colon U \to \mathbf{C}$ be the two branches of the square root of $1 - 4c$. There is no problem in defining the branches since $1/4 \notin U$ and U is simply connected. Then $f_n(c)$ omits (for instance) the three points:

$$h_1(c) = 1/2 + g_1(c), \quad h_2(c) = 1/2 + g_2(c) \quad \text{and} \quad \infty.$$

The two points $h_1(c)$ and $h_2(c)$ are the fixed points (which only coincide for $c = 1/4$). We obtain a family $F_n \colon U \to \bar{\mathbf{C}}$ which omits 0, 1, ∞ by composing with the affine transformation which is uniquely determined by mapping the three points onto 0, 1, ∞ respectively. Hence

$$F_n = \frac{f_n - h_1}{h_2 - h_1}.$$

The family $\{F_n \colon U \to \bar{\mathbf{C}}\}$ is normal and so is the family $\{f_n \colon U \to \mathbf{C}\}$, which is a contradiction. We have in fact proved that the set of Misiurewicz points for which 0 is eventually mapped onto a fixed point is dense in the boundary.

The second statement above is proved in the same way. We assume that it is false and choose U to be a simply connected neighborhood of c_0 so that U contains no centers of hyperbolic components. Let $g_1, g_2 \colon U \to \mathbf{C}$ be the two branches of the square root of $-c$. Then $f_n(c)$ omits the three points: 0, $g_1(c)$, $g_2(c)$, which leads to a contradiction.

Local similarity between the Mandelbrot set and Julia sets. We have seen that the Misiurewicz points are dense in the boundary of M. Tan Lei [T] has proved that there exists a similarity between the Julia set and the Mandelbrot set around every Misiurewicz point c; that means that looking in a strong microscope at a neighborhood of c in either the dynamical plane

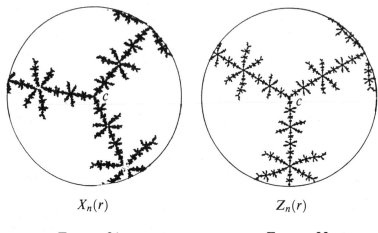

$$X_n(r) \qquad\qquad\qquad Z_n(r)$$

FIGURE 21   FIGURE 22

or the parameter plane the Julia set and the Mandelbrot set look the same, up to a rotation. The precise statement is the following:

Let l be the smallest integer such that $x_j = P_c^{\circ j}(0)$ is periodic, say of period k, and let ρ be the multiplier of the periodic orbit $\{x_l, \ldots, x_{l+k-1}\}$. Translate—in the dynamical plane—the Julia set so that c is placed at 0: $\tau_c(J_c)$. Multiply the translated Julia set by ρ^n and look at the part within a disc D_r of radius r, for any chosen $r > 0$, union the boundary of the disc:

$$X_n(r) = [D_r \cap \rho^n(\tau_c(J_c))] \cup \partial D_r.$$

Translate—in the parameter plane—the Mandelbrot set so that c is placed at 0: $\tau_c(M)$. Multiply the translated Mandelbrot set by ρ^n:

$$Y_n(r) = \rho^n(\tau_c(M)).$$

There exists a $\lambda_c \neq 0$ such that the Hausdorff distance between the sets

$$X_n(r) \text{ and } Z_n(r) = [D_r \cap \lambda_c Y_n(r)] \cup \partial D_r$$

tends to 0 when n tends to ∞.

Figure 21 shows a blow up of the Julia set for the Misiurewicz point $c \approx -0.101096 + i0.956287$ around c (compare with Figure 15). Figure 22 shows a blow up of the Mandelbrot set around the same Misiurewicz point.

10. The universality of the Mandelbrot set. Copies of the Mandelbrot set are found not only in the parameter plane for quadratic polynomials, but in many other one-parameter families of analytic mappings. The reason is that the mappings (or some iterates thereof) locally may behave as a quadratic polynomial. This is explained by A. Douady and J. H. Hubbard in their paper about polynomial-like mappings [DH3].

An analytic map

$$f: U' \to U$$

is called *polynomial-like* of degree d if U, U' are open subsets of $\mathbf{C}$ isomorphic to discs, with $\overline{U}' \subset U$, and if f is proper of degree d.

Consider a one-parameter family Λ, isomorphic to a disc, of polynomial-like mappings of degree 2:

$$f_\lambda \colon U'_\lambda \to U_\lambda, \qquad \lambda \in \Lambda.$$

There is a unique critical point $\omega_\lambda \in U'_\lambda$. One can prove that Λ contains a copy of the Mandelbrot set if there exists a closed subset $A \subset \Lambda$, A isomorphic to $\overline{D}$, such that $f_\lambda(\omega_\lambda) \in U_\lambda - U'_\lambda$ for all $\lambda \in \Lambda - \mathrm{int}(A)$, and such that $f_\lambda(\omega_\lambda) - \omega_\lambda$ turns around 0 once when λ describes the boundary of A, see Figure 23.

$$\lambda \in \Lambda - \mathrm{inf}(A)$$

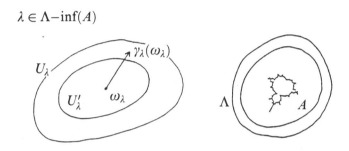

Dynamical plane   Parameter plane

FIGURE 23

Using this result one can understand why we see small copies of the Mandelbrot set inside itself. The polynomial-like mappings of degree 2 are in these cases restrictions of $P_c^{\circ k}$ for an appropriate k to an appropriate subset U'.

Moreover, one can prove that the different decorations surrounding the small copies of M inside the Mandelbrot set always have a binary structure. The decorations are attached to the small copy of M at the points which correspond to the points $\gamma_M(p/2^k)$ in the complete Mandelbrot set. Compare with the Colored Plates 1–3 and 4–6. Detect first the decorations attached to the points corresponding to $\gamma_M(0)$ and $\gamma_M(1/2)$, then $\gamma_M(1/2^2)$ and $\gamma_M(3/2^2)$, etc.

Finally we give an example of a one-parameter family of analytic mappings obtained from Newton's method for finding roots of a cubic polynomial.

Newton's iteration applied to a function f is defined as follows: If we know an approximate solution x_0 of the equation $f(x) = 0$, sufficiently close to an actual solution a, then we can obtain a better approximation x_1 to a by computing

$$x_1 = x_0 - \frac{f(x_0)}{f'(x_0)}.$$

Iterating this process leads to a sequence of numbers x_n which converges extremely fast towards a. If we do not start the iteration "sufficiently close" to the solution a the sequence might not converge towards a but to another solution or it might not converge at all to a solution of $f(x) = 0$. In order to try to understand Newton's method we ask the following question: what happens in the long run if we start the iteration at an arbitrary seed z_0.

In particular let P_λ denote the cubic polynomial of the form

$$P_\lambda(z) = (z - 1)(z + 1/2 - \lambda)(z + 1/2 + \lambda)$$

with the roots 1, $-1/2 - \lambda$, $-1/2 + \lambda$ which we shall refer to as the red, blue and green root respectively. The form of the polynomial is chosen so that the roots add up to 0. It follows that the point 0 is the unique inflection point of P_λ; i.e. $P_\lambda''(0) = 0$. Newton's iteration applied to the polynomial P_λ is iteration by the rational map

$$N_\lambda(z) = z - \frac{P_\lambda(z)}{P_\lambda'(z)}$$

with critical points: the roots and the inflection point.

It is easy to show that the rational map associated to an arbitrary cubic polynomial with more than one root is conjugated by a Möbius transformation to N_λ for some λ.

A seed z_0 might under iteration by N_λ be attracted to one of the roots of P_λ and we will color the seed red, blue or green corresponding to the root to which it is being attracted and make the color darker or lighter measuring the number of iterations it takes to get close to this root (see Colored Plates 4–6 in the article by Keen). A seed z_0 might belong to the Julia set of N_λ in which case it is not attracted to a root.

For some polynomials something else can happen: a seed z_0 might be attracted to a cycle which is not a root. If so we will color the seed yellow. In Color Plate 6 in the article by Keen we see that the yellow patterns reproduce filled-in Julia sets of quadratic polynomials. Moreover, if N_λ has an attracting cycle different from the roots, then it must attract 0 since it must attract a critical point.

For each N_λ there is only one interesting critical orbit to follow, namely the orbit of 0. In the λ-parameter plane we color λ red, blue or green if 0 is being attracted to the corresponding root and yellow otherwise. In the parameter plane we see small yellow copies of the Mandelbrot set (see Color Plate 12). That each one really is a homeomorphic image of the Mandelbrot set is proved by using the theory of polynomial-like mappings.

It is this astonishing universality of the Mandelbrot set which makes it so important.

BIBLIOGRAPHY

[Bl] P. Blanchard, *Complex analytic dynamics on the Riemann sphere*, Bull. Amer. Math. Soc. **11** (1984), 85–141.

[BD] B. Branner and A. Douady, *Surgery on complex polynomials*, Proceedings of the Symposium on Dynamical Systems, Mexico, 1986, Lecture Notes in Math., vol. 1345, Springer (to appear).

[BH1] B. Branner and J. H. Hubbard, *The iteration of cubic polynomials Part I: The global topology of parameter space*, Acta Math. **160** (1988), 143–206.

[BH2] B. Branner and J. H. Hubbard, *The iteration of cubic polynomials, Part II: Patterns and parapatterns*, Preprint, 1989.

[BM] R. Brooks and J. P. Matelski, *The dynamics of 2-generator subgroups of* PSL(2, **C**), Proceedings of the 1978 Stony Brook Conference: Riemann Surfaces and Related Topics, Ann. of Math. Stud. **97**, 1980, 65–71.

[Br] H. Brolin, *Invariant sets under iteration of rational functions*, Ark. Mat. **6** (1965), 103–144.

[C] A. Cayley, *The Newton-Fourier imaginary problem*, Amer. J. Math. **2** (1879), 97.

[D1] A. Douady, *Systèmes dynamiques holomorphes*, Sém. Bourbaki, 35e anné, #599; Astérisque 105–106, 1983, 39–63.

[D2] A. Douady, *Julia sets and the Mandelbrot set*, in [PR]: The Beauty of Fractals, Springer-Verlag, 1986, 161–173.

[DH1] A. Douady and J. H. Hubbard, *Itération des polynômes quadratiques complexes*, C. R. Acad. Sci. **294** (1982), 123–126.

[DH2] A. Douady and J. H. Hubbard, *Étude dynamique des polynômes complexes*, I, II, Publ. Math. Orsay, 1984, 1985.

[DH3] A. Douady and J. H. Hubbard, *On the dynamics of polynomial-like mappings*, Ann. Sci. École Norm. Sup. (4) **18** (1985), 287–343.

[F] P. Fatou, *Mémoire sur les équatios fonctionnelles*, Bull. Soc. Math. France **47** (1919), 161–271; **47** (1920), 33–94 and 208–314.

[Fi] Y. Fisher, *Exploring the Mandelbrot set*, Appendix D in The Science of Fractals, edited by H.-O. Peitgen and D. Saupe, Springer-Verlag, 1988, 287–296.

[K] L. Keen, *Julia sets*, in this volume.

[J] G. Julia, *Mémoires sur l'iteration des fonctions rationnelles*, J. Math. Pures Appl. **8** (1918), 47–245.

[L1] P. Lavaurs, *Une description combinatoire de l'involution définie par M sur les rationnels à dénominateur impair*, C. R. Acad Sci. (4) **303** (1986), 143–146.

[L2] P. Lavaurs, *Le lieu de connexité des polynômes du troisième degré n'est pas localement connexe*, manuscript, 1986.

[L3] P. Lavaurs, *Complément à une inégalité de Yoccoz*, manuscript, 1986.

[Ma] B. B. Mandelbrot, *Fractals and the rebirth of iteration theory*, in [PR]: The Beauty of Fractals, Springer-Verlag, 1966, 151–160.

[M1] J. Milnor, *Self-similarity and hairiness in the Mandelbrot set*, Computers in Geometry and Topology, edited by M. Tangora, Marcel Dekker (to appear).

[M2] J. Milnor, *Remarks on iterated cubic maps*, manuscript, 1986.

[M3] J. Milnor, *Hyperbolic components in spaces of polynomial maps*, manuscript, 1987.

[Mo] R. Monafo, *Super MANDELZOOM*, program for the Macintosh. Public domain.

[MSS] R. Mañe, P. Sad and D. Sullivan, *On the dynamics of rational maps*, Ann. Sci. École. Norm Sup. (4) **16** (1983), 193–217.

[PR] H.-O. Peitgen and P. Richter, *The beauty of fractals*, Springer-Verlag, 1986.

[Si] C. L. Siegel, *Iteration of analytic functions*, Ann. of Math. (2) **43** (1942), 607–612.

[T] Tan Lei, *Ressemblance entre l'ensemble de Mandelbrot et l'ensemble de Julia au voisinage d'un point de Misiurewicz*, in [DH2] II, 139–152.

[Y] J.-C. Yoccoz, *Sur la taille des membres de l'ensemble de Mandelbrot*, manuscript, 1986.

MATHEMATICAL INSTITUTE, THE TECHNICAL UNIVERSITY OF DENMARK, DK-2800 LYNGBY, DENMARK

Proceedings of Symposia in Applied Mathematics
Volume **39**, 1989

An Introduction to Fractals

JENNY HARRISON

1. Introduction. The advent of the computer and easy graphical analysis has spurred a broad, public interest in fractals. As mathematicians, we ask, 'Are fractals relevant to our mathematical and physical worlds?' The answer is not simple as this is a subject with both history and new beginnings. Some problems have been solved and others have not even been imagined. Mathematical theories take time in the making, but some have been quietly developing. There are already ties with dynamical systems, geometry, complexity theory, and number theory, to name just a few.

Hausdorff's definitions of Hausdorff measure and dimension in 1919 marked the beginning of the study of geometric measure theory as in the volumes of Besicovitch and Federer. There is much to learn from these works. They provide a valuable mathematical foundation. A bifurcation point in the study of dimension came when Mandelbrot (1975, 1977, 1982) pioneered the use of sets with fractional dimension to model scientific phenomena from the molecular to the galactic. In this sense, 'fractal theory' is a new subject.

These notes have several goals. One is to survey some of the useful techniques from geometric measure theory, especially aids in computation. Proofs are generally not given, but substantial references are used. (Falconer (1985) is excellent.) We highlight two common classes of examples of fractals: self-similar sets and quasi-circles. Finally, we discuss the relevance of fractals in calculus.

We assume knowledge of concepts in a standard real analysis course (as in Rudin). We work in Euclidean space $\mathbf{R}^n$, although much of what is said is valid in a more general metric space setting.

The author wishes to thank Jaroslav Stark for his help with the graphics.

1980 *Mathematics Subject Classification* (1985 *Revision*). Primary 28Dxx.

2. Preliminaries. Mandelbrot defined a fractal to be a set with Hausdorff dimension strictly larger than its topological dimension. (The topological dimension of a set is always bounded above by its Hausdorff dimension.) He pointed out that the definition is not completely satisfactory as it excludes some highly irregular sets in the spirit of fractals. In the past, these sets were referred to as 'sets of fractional dimension', 'sets of Hausdorff measure' or 'irregular sets'.

Hausdorff measure is often hard to compute, but this is tolerated because the Hausdorff measure is a genuine measure (i.e. additive on a countable collection of disjoint sets). There have been a number of variations of the definition which don't always lead to a proper measure. Hausdorff dimension is by far the most commonly used.

2.1. Hausdorff dimension. Topological dimension is a whole number defined for certain sets. Curves have dimension 1, surfaces have dimension 2 and solids have 3 dimensions. (See Hurewicz and Wallman (1941) for a rigorous definition.) Topological dimension is what most of us think of as the 'natural dimension'. It is invariant under homeomorphisms. That is, if the topological dimension of E is k then the topological dimension of $h(E)$ is also k if h is a homeomorphism.

The Hausdorff dimension is defined for any subset of $\mathbf{R}^n$ that you can probably imagine. This includes all open sets, closed sets, countable unions of closed sets, countable intersections of open sets, etc. (See Rogers (1970) or Falconer (1985).) It will follow easily from the definition that Hausdorff dimension is not invariant under homeomorphisms. However, the topological dimension of E is the infimum of the Hausdorff dimensions of its homeomorphic images $h(E)$. Later we will discover that Hausdorff dimension is invariant under something slightly stronger—quasi-isometries (sometimes called 'bi-Lipschitz maps' or 'Lipeomorphic maps'). Indeed, we will see that the equivalence class of quasi-isometric self-similar curves is completely determined by Hausdorff dimension!

Now a word about the definition. It is not short and easy. Much like the definitions of differential forms and entropy, it takes thought and practice to truly understand it. You don't have to know the actual definition to appreciate the pictures or to have a feeling for what it means for the dimension to increase, say. But if you want to work with it you may very well find that you need the rigorous definition in all its detail. There are several methods for calculating the dimension which avoid the definition, some of which will be given in this exposition.

If $x = (x_1, x_2, \ldots, x_n) \in \mathbf{R}^n$, define $|x| = \sqrt{x_1^2 + x_2^2 + \cdots + x_n^2}$, the Euclidean *norm* of x.

If U is a nonempty subset of $\mathbf{R}^n$ we define the *diameter* of U as

$$|U| = \sup\{|x - y| : x, y \in U\}.$$

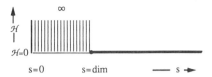

FIGURE 1. The graph of $H^s(E)$.

If $E \subset \bigcup_i U_i$ and $0 < |U_i| \le \delta$ for each i, we say that $\{U_i\}$ is a δ-cover of E.

Let $E \subset \mathbf{R}^n$ and let s be a nonnegative number. For $\delta > 0$, define

$$\mathcal{H}_\delta^s(E) = \inf \sum_{i=1}^{\infty} |U_i|^s$$

where the infimum is over all δ-covers $\{U_i\}$ of E. The limit of $\mathcal{H}_\delta^s(E)$ as $\delta \to 0$ is the *s-dimensional Hausdorff outer measure* of E, $\mathcal{H}^s(E)$. Call $E \subset \mathbf{R}^n$ $\mathcal{H}^s$-*measurable* if $\mathcal{H}^s(T) = \mathcal{H}^s(T \cap E) + \mathcal{H}^s(T \backslash E)$ for all $T \subset \mathbf{R}^n$. (In practice, most current applications deal with closed sets, all of which are $\mathcal{H}^s$-measurable.) Now restrict $\mathcal{H}^s$ to the $\mathcal{H}^s$-measurable sets to obtain the *s-dimensional Hausdorff measure*, or simply, *s-measure*. This restriction guarantees that the s-measure behaves well. In particular the s-measure of a countable union of disjoint sets is precisely the sum of the s-measures of the sets. This is clearly desirable.

The definition of s-dimensional Hausdorff measure is similar to that of n-dimensional Lebesgue measure except that diameters to the power s are used in the sums. In Euclidean space $\mathbf{R}^n$, the n-dimensional Lebesgue measure $\mathcal{L}^n$ is a constant multiple of Hausdorff n-measure. Thus $\mathcal{H}^s$ agrees with the usual notions of s-dimensional volume in case s is an integer.

The most important concept to focus on in the definition of s-measure is 'inf'. You want to get the smallest sum you can. Clearly, you should avoid overlaps. If you were allowed to have large disks U_i in your cover, then you could cover up a 'messy' patch with one shot and avoid a large contribution to the sum. The restriction that the diameter $\delta \to 0$ requires you to take into account finer and finer detail that might not be apparent in the larger scale. Thus $\mathcal{H}_\delta^s$ increases as δ decreases.

Now let s vary. Clearly, $\mathcal{H}^s(E)$ decreases as s increases. For large s $\mathcal{H}^s(E)$ is 0.

Define the *Hausdorff dimension* of E by

$$\dim(E) = \inf\{s: \mathcal{H}^s(E) = 0\}.$$

You can verify that $\dim(E) = \sup\{s: \mathcal{H}^s(E) = \infty\}$.

If you draw a graph of $\mathcal{H}^s(E)$ as a function of s, you can see that the Hausdorff dimension of E is the unique point where the values $\mathcal{H}^s(E)$ jump from ∞ to 0. See Figure 1.

It would be an excellent exercise at this point for the reader to show that the Hausdorff dimension of the Cantor middle set is $\log 2 / \log 3$, using the definition. You will find that it is easy to show that $\log 2 / \log 3$ is an upper bound of the dimension. Your work will come in showing that it is also a lower bound. (See Falconer pp. 14–15 if you need help!)

Henceforth we write *dimension* instead of *Hausdorff dimension*, unless otherwise stated.

2.2. Local structure of fractals. $E \subset \mathbf{R}^n$ is called an *s-set* if $0 < \mathscr{H}^s(E) < \infty$. (It follows automatically that $\dim(E) = s$.) For $x \in \mathbf{R}^n$ let

$$B_\delta(x) = \{y \in \mathbf{R}^n : |x - y| < \delta\}.$$

E has *locally finite s-measure* if whenever $x \in \operatorname{clos}(E)$ there exists $\delta > 0$ such that $\mathscr{H}^s(B_\delta(x) \cap E) < \infty$. E has *locally positive s-measure* if $\mathscr{H}^s(B_\delta(x) \cap E) > 0$ for all $x \in E$ and $\delta > 0$.

The existence of a locally finite, positive s-measure for an arbitrary set provides a structure somewhat analogous to the coordinate charts of a manifold. The assumption of locally positive measure guarantees homogeneity of dimension. Where the measure is 0, the dimension might be smaller—think of a snowflake (see §4) with some straight segments glued in. The assumption of local finiteness can give essential control of estimates. Together, these assumptions often give enough local structure to prove good theorems.

2.3. Alternate definitions. There are many other definitions of dimension, although Hausdorff dimension is the most commonly used. Tricot (1981) did a study of 12 definitions of dimension! Most definitions have some restriction on the δ-covers considered in the definition of measure. In some situations these definitions are more natural for the application (see Yomdin (1983), for example). Sometimes it is just too hard to find the Hausdorff dimension, but possible for other definitions. We briefly consider the most common alternative.

BOX DIMENSION.[1] Box dimension is defined in the same way as Hausdorff dimension except that in the definition of measure only disks in $\mathbf{R}^n$ of the same radius δ are considered for covers of E. It follows that box dimension is always $\geq$ Hausdorff dimension. Although it is fairly easy to work with, it has the unfortunate property of 'respecting closure'. That is, the box dimension of the closure of a set is the same as for the set itself. Thus the box dimension of the rationals is 1. We would really like any definition of dimension to be countably additive and recommend that box dimension be used only for closed sets. Even for compact sets it can differ from Hausdorff dimension. On the other hand there are situations where box dimension gives the most natural result. (See Yomdin (1983), for example.)

2.4. Comparable net measures. Next we will see a useful method which simplifies the task of computing the Hausdorff measure. It enables one to

---

[1]Kolmogorov first defined this in 1961 and called it entropy dimension. H is often called capacity or outer capacity.

avoid considering all possible covers of a set when computing the Hausdorff measure—usually a daunting prospect.

A collection of sets $\mathcal{N}$ is a *net* if whenever $B_1, B_2 \in \mathcal{N}$ then either $B_1 \cap B_2 = \varnothing$ or $B_1 \subset B_2$. In addition, we require that each set in $\mathcal{N}$ is contained in only finitely many others. It follows that any collection of sets of $\mathcal{N}$ has a disjoint subcollection with the same union—simply remove the sets which are contained in others.

In order to define the s-net measure $\mathcal{M}^s$ on $\mathbf{R}^n$, we define $\mathcal{N}_r$ to be the net consisting of the half-open grid of $\mathbf{R}^n$ of width r^{-k}, $r \geq 2$ being an integer. Specifically, $\mathcal{N}_r$ consists of cubes of the form

$$[r^{-k}t_1, r^{-k}(t_1 + 1)) \times [r^{-k}t_2, r^{-k}(t_2 + 1)) \times \cdots \times [r^{-k}t_n, r^{-k}(t_n + 1))$$

where the t_i and k are integers, $k \geq 0$. $\mathcal{N}_2$ is called the *binary grid*.

For $E \subset \mathbf{R}^n$ define

$$\mathcal{M}_r^s(E) = \liminf_{\delta \to 0} \sum_{i=1}^{\infty} |S_i|^s$$

where the infimum is taken over all countable δ-covers of E by cubes S_i of $\mathcal{N}_r$.

You can see that the net measure is defined in the same way as Hausdorff s-measure except that only elements from the r^{-k} grid are used for the sums.

It is remarkable that net measure is 'comparable' to Hausdorff measure as shown in the following theorem.

THEOREM. *There exists a constant C depending only on r and the dimension n such that for every $E \subset \mathbf{R}^n$*

$$\mathcal{H}^s(E) \leq \mathcal{M}_r^s(E) \leq C\mathcal{H}^s(E).$$

The first inequality follows immediately from the definitions since Hausdorff measures are found using all covers, not just r^{-k} grids. The second inequality is not so obvious. See Falconer for a proof for binary grids.

This theorem immediately implies that Hausdorff dimension may be found using net measures since $\inf\{s : \mathcal{H}^s(E) = 0\} = \inf\{s : \mathcal{M}_r^s(E) = 0\}$.

Recall from your work on the Cantor set that it is harder to find lower bounds for Hausdorff dimension than upper bounds. A natural way to approach the problem would be to first guess a lower bound s for the dimension of E and then show its Hausdorff s-measure is positive. Hence $\dim(E) \geq s$. With this theorem, you only have to estimate your measure over the net $\mathcal{N}_r$: If the net-measure $\mathcal{M}_r^s$ is positive then so is the Hausdorff s-measure.

For practice, you might try to use this theorem to quickly prove that $\log 2 / \log 3$ is a lower bound for the dimension of the middle third Cantor set.

2.5. Density for fractals. You may recall the Lebesgue density theorem:

THEOREM. *Let E be a Lebesgue measurable subset of* $\mathbf{R}^n$. *Then the Lebesgue density of E at x,*

$$\lim_{r\to 0} \frac{\mathscr{L}^n(E \cap B_r(x))}{\mathscr{L}^n(B_r(x))},$$

exists and equals 1 *if* $x \in E$ *and* 0 *if* $x \notin E$, *except for a subset of* $\mathbf{R}^n$ *with* $\mathscr{L}^n$-*measure* 0.

If it exists, the limit is the *density* of $\mathscr{L}^n$ at x. The Lebesgue density theorem tells us that the Lebesgue measure is evenly spread out. This is not the case for Hausdorff measures.

The *lower (upper) s-dimensional density* of E at x is defined to be, respectively

$$\liminf_{r\to 0} \frac{\mathscr{H}^s(E \cap B_r(x))}{r^s},$$

$$\limsup_{r\to 0} \frac{\mathscr{H}^s(E \cap B_r(x))}{r^s}.$$

If these quantities are positive and finite then E has *bounded density* at x. (We will see in §4 that self-similar curves such as the snowflake have bounded density.) If they are equal, their value is the *s-dimensional density* of E at x.

THEOREM (MARSTRAND (1954)). *If* E *is an s-set with* $0 < s < 1$ *the s-dimensional density of* E *fails to exist at almost every point of* E.

Here, 'almost every' means 'except for a set with s-measure 0'.

However, in practice, one does not always need the density to exist. Inequalities provided by the upper and lower densities will often suffice.

Hutchinson (1981) contains a further discussion of density.

3. Self-similar fractals. We now turn to some special types of fractals which commonly arise in both computer graphics and mathematical constructions. The simplest kind are called self-similar sets. They are built from pieces similar to the entire set but on a finer and finer scale. In Mandelbrot (1977) such sets are constructed by an iterative process using an initial and standard polygon. Hutchinson (1981) has generalized the process and we present his method below.

3.1. Fractal approximations of compact sets. A *contraction* is a mapping S satisfying $|S(x) - S(y)| \leq C|x - y|$ for all $x, y \in \mathbf{R}^n$ where $C < 1$. The infimum of all C for which this inequality holds is called the *contraction ratio*. A compact set $E \subset \mathbf{R}^n$ is *invariant* for a finite set $\mathscr{S} = \{S_1, S_2, \ldots, S_m\}$ of contraction maps on $\mathbf{R}^n$ if $E = \bigcup_i S_i(E)$. A contraction is *rigid* if $|S(x) - S(y)| = r|x - y|$ for some $0 < r < 1$. The contraction ratio is simply r, the amount of contraction.

We will see that for any finite set of contraction maps $\mathscr{S}$, there exists a unique compact set E invariant under $\mathscr{S}$.

For $x \in \mathbf{R}^n$ and $E \subset \mathbf{R}^n$ define the *distance* from x to E to be

$$d(x, E) = \inf\{|x - y| : y \in E\}.$$

Define the *Hausdorff metric* δ on pairs of nonempty compact subsets of $\mathbf{R}^n$ by

$$\delta(E, F) = \sup\{d(x, F), d(y, E) . x \in E, y \in F\}.$$

The space of all compact, nonempty subsets of $\mathbf{R}^n$ is a metric space $\mathcal{H}$ respecting this metric δ. It shares many properties with $\mathbf{R}^n$. It is complete (respecting δ), locally compact, connected and locally connected. The map $S : E \mapsto \bigcup_i S_i(E)$ turns out to be a contraction of $\mathcal{H}$. The fixed point of S, say K, is an invariant set for the contractions $\{S_i\}$. The $\{S_i\}$ are said to *generate* K. Formally,

THEOREM. *Let* $\mathcal{S} = \{S_1, \ldots, S_m\}$ *be a finite set of contraction maps on* $\mathbf{R}^n$. *Then there exists a unique compact set* K *such that*

$$K = S(K) = \bigcup_{i=1}^{m} S_i(K).$$

Furthermore, if F *is any nonempty compact subset of* $\mathbf{R}^n$ *the iterates* $S^k(F)$ *converge to* K *in the Hausdorff metric as* $k \to \infty$.

The last assertion holds simply because K is an attracting fixed point of S.

Notice that since a single point x is compact this theorem says that its iterates $S^k(x)$ converge to K in the Hausdorff metric. Note, too, that $S(x)$ is a set whereas x is a point; $S^k(x)$ has $\leq m^k$ elements. In practice, that means if you know the contraction maps which generate K, a subset of $\mathbf{R}^2$, say, then you can draw K on a computer screen by plotting $S^k(x)$ and ignoring the first 1000 or so points drawn. Since the number of points in $S^k(x)$ may grow exponentially, it is only practical to plot a subsequence of the orbit.

The next question is—given a compact set E, how do you actually find a set of contraction mappings which generate E? Well, you may not be able to do this, but you can come close. Let E be a compact set contained in the unit square of $\mathbf{R}^2$ and $\varepsilon > 0$. E is covered with finitely many squares from the ε-grid of $\mathbf{R}^2$. For each of these squares A_i, there is an affine contraction which takes the unit square onto A_i. Then choose any point in the unit square, iterate it and plot the long term points. These points will converge to a compact set K within ε of E. Furthermore, this set K will be self-similar. (See below.)

The problem is that if E has complicated small detail then this naïve approach will require very small disks and hence enormous computer power to capture the details. The challenge of finding a more efficient algorithm has been the subject of Barnsley's investigations. (See his notes in this Short Course. It should be noted, that, to date, Barnsley's efficiency methods have not been disclosed.)

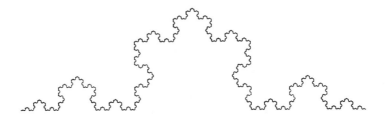

FIGURE 2. dim $= \frac{\log 4}{\log 3} = 1.2619\ldots$. The Koch curve.

3.2. Self-similar sets. Let K be the invariant set for $\{S_i\}$ and let $\{r_i\}$ be the contraction ratios. The *similarity dimension* of K is the unique positive number s such that

$$\sum_{i=1}^{m} r_i^s = 1.$$

This number is well defined—it doesn't depend on the contraction maps generating K—and it is easily calculable.

A *similitude* is the composition of a translation and a homothety.

If the r_i are similitudes and $\mathscr{H}^s(S_i(E) \cap S_j(E)) = 0$ $(i \neq j)$ then K is called self-similar. (Without this extra condition, the self-similarity would be lost in the overlaps.)

THEOREM. *If K is self-similar then the Hausdorff dimension of K is the same as its similarity dimension.*

EXAMPLES. (1) The middle third Cantor set is obtained as the compact set invariant under the similitudes $S_1(x) = x/3$ and $S_2(x) = (x+2)/3$. Hence its Hausdorff dimension is $\log 2/\log 3$. As an exercise, you might devise a simple computer program to draw the Cantor set in the above manner—begin with $x = 1$, for example and use a random number generator to dictate whether you should apply S_1 or S_2 to plot the successive points on the screen.

(2) The classic 'snowflake' or Koch curve is pictured in Figure 2. It is generated by the four homotheties depicted. Their contraction ratios are each $1/3$. By the theorem, the Hausdorff dimension of the snowflake is $s = \log 4/\log 3$ since $r_1 = r_2 = r_3 = r_4 = 1/3$.

(3) Variants of the snowflake (Figure 3). It is possible to draw a continuum of examples similar to the snowflake with Hausdorff dimension varying between 1 and 2. We give one example with dimension 1.5.

(4) The Peano curve, or 'space-filling curve', has dimension 2 (see Figure 4). It represents the upper limit of this continuum of examples in the plane. Note that it has many self-intersections.

3.3. Lipschitz equivalence of self-similar curves. A mapping $f\colon M \to M$ is called a *homeomorphism* if f is invertible and both f and f^{-1} are continuous. If both f and its inverse are C^1 then f is called a *diffeomorphism*.

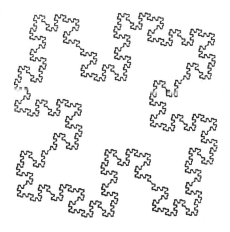

FIGURE 3. dim $= \frac{\log 8}{\log 4} = 1.5.$

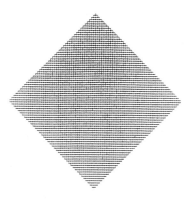

FIGURE 4. dim $= \frac{\log 9}{\log 3} = 2.$ The Peano curve.

A mapping $f: \mathbf{R}^n \to \mathbf{R}^m$ is said to be *Lipschitz* if there exists a constant $K > 0$ such that $|f(x) - f(y)| \le K|x - y|$ for $x, y \in \mathbf{R}^n$. If f is invertible and f^{-1} is Lipschitz then f is called a *quasi-isometry*. Subsets $P \subset \mathbf{R}^n$ and $Q \subset \mathbf{R}^m$ are said to be *quasi-isometric* if there exists a quasi-isometry $f: P \to Q$. Quasi-isometries are special kinds of homeomorphisms. Diffeomorphisms are special kinds of quasi-isometries. It is easy to see from the definitions that if two sets are quasi-isometric then they have the same dimension. Falconer pointed out to me the remarkable 'folk theorem' that the converse is true for self-similar sets.

THEOREM. *Two self-similar arcs P and Q are quasi-isometric if and only if* $\dim(P) = \dim(Q)$.

The proof is worth understanding for its principles are basic and commonly arise. Suppose $\dim(P) = \dim(Q) = s$. It is not hard to show that all the subarcs of P and Q are s-sets since P and Q are self-similar. Hence their s-measures are locally positive and finite. Use the measure $\mathcal{H}^s$ to parametrize P and Q: Let $a \in \mathbf{R}^n$ be the initial point of P and $b \in \mathbf{R}^m$ the initial point of Q. Let $x \in P$. The arc connecting a and x has measure c. Let $f(x)$ be the unique point in Q such that the s-measure of the arc connecting b with $f(x)$ has s-measure c. Since P and Q are self-similar, their upper and lower densities, U and L, are positive and finite at every point. Let γ_1 denote the arc connecting x and y in P and γ_2 the arc connecting $f(x)$ and $f(y)$ in Q. Then

$$|f(x) - f(y)|^s \leq \frac{\mathcal{H}^s(\gamma_2)}{L_Q} = \frac{\mathcal{H}^s(\gamma_1)}{L_Q} \leq \frac{U_P}{L_Q}|x - y|^s.$$

Taking the s-root, we see that f is Lipschitz. The proof that f^{-1} is Lipschitz is similar.

REMARKS. (1) It is not known if the quasi-isometry f extends to a neighborhood of P.

(2) The proof can be easily generalized to arcs which have bounded density.

3.4. Quasi-circles. A Jordan curve Q is called a *quasi-circle* if there exists a constant $K > 0$ such that for every $x, y \in Q$ one of the arcs of Q connecting x and y has diameter $\leq K|x - y|$. (An arc is a *quasi-arc* if it has the same property.) A quasi-circle is a Jordan curve without too much pinching—its 'bays have wide mouths'. (See Figure 5.)

FIGURE 5. A quasi-circle.

Quasi-circles occur commonly in mathematics. For example, Julia sets of expanding rational maps which are known to be Jordan curves are quasi-circles. (See Sullivan's preprints.) Ruelle (1982) proved that the Julia set Q for $z \mapsto z^2 + c$ has dimension $1 + |c|^2/4\log 2 +$ higher order terms if $|c| < 1$. Furthermore, for sufficiently small $|c|$, Q is a quasi-circle. The snowflake is a quasi-circle. Indeed, all self-similar Jordan curves are quasi-circles.

The next fractal pictured below is an example of a quasi-arc which is not self-similar. (Although it is 'quasi self-similar'.) The method used to generate this arc is applicable to any nonrepeating sequence of real numbers. (See Harrison (1988b).) The arc depicted is generated by the sequence $n\alpha$ (mod 1) where $\alpha = (\sqrt{5} - 1)/2$, the Golden Mean. Following it are several other curves produced with the same algorithm. The geometry of these curves Q is so closely tied to the continued fraction expansion of α that we call Q a *continued fractal.* (See Figure 6; and Figures 7 and 8 on page 118.)

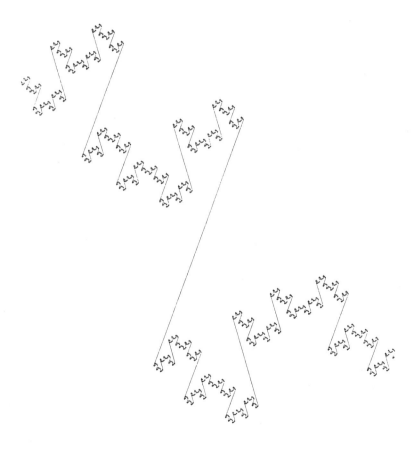

FIGURE 6.   The continued fractal generated by the Golden Mean.

FIGURE 7. The continued fractal generated by $\alpha = \pi/2$
(detail).

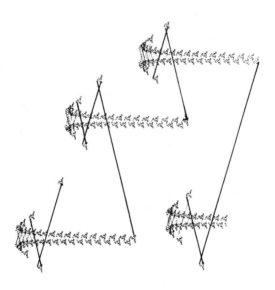

FIGURE 8. The continued fractal generated by $\alpha = 2^{1/4}$
(detail).

4. Fractals in calculus. If we wish to understand how fractals affect the mathematical and physical worlds, it is useful to first understand their relation to calculus.

4.1. Graphs of continuous functions. The graph Γ of a smooth function $f: \mathbf{R} \to \mathbf{R}$ is as smooth as the function f. Thus if f is C^1 we know that $\dim(\Gamma) = 1$. What if f is only continuous? Its graph is continuous, but may well be a fractal. Its dimension is controlled by the differentiability of f.

A function $f: \mathbf{R} \to \mathbf{R}$ is of class C^ε, $0 < \varepsilon < 1$, if there exist constants $C > 0$ and $\delta > 0$ such that

$$|f(x + h) - f(x)| \le Ch^\varepsilon$$

for all x, y with $|x - y| \le \delta$. (f is sometimes said to be a *Hölder* function of class ε.)

THEOREM (BESICOVITCH AND URSELL (1937)). *If $f: \mathbf{R} \to \mathbf{R}$ is of class C^ε then $\dim(\Gamma) \le 2 - \varepsilon$.*

This result is 'sharp'. Besicovitch and Ursell found functions which are of class C^ε and whose graphs have dimension $2 - \varepsilon$.

The Weierstrass functions

$$f(x) = \sum_{i=1}^{\infty} \frac{\sin(\lambda^i x)}{\lambda^{\varepsilon i}}$$

are closely related; $\lambda > 1$ and $0 < \varepsilon < 1$ are constants (see Figure 9.) It is of class C^ε. It seems likely that the dimension of the graph of f is $2 - \varepsilon$ but this has not been proved rigorously. (Mandelbrot (1977), and Berry and Lewis (1980) have studied variants of this function with computer experiments.)

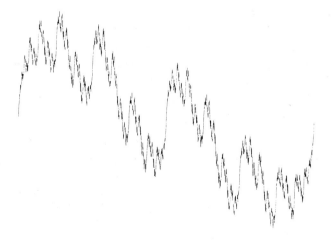

FIGURE 9. The Weierstrass function for $\lambda = 2$, $\varepsilon = .5$, $\dim = 1.5$.

4.2. The Morse-Sard theorem. We next turn to an interesting class of examples first discovered by Whitney (1935) and extended to all self-similar arcs by Norton (1987).

Let E be any self-similar arc in $\mathbf{R}^n$ (such as the snowflake) with $\dim(E) = s > 1$. Choose an 'initial' point $a \in E$. Define a real valued function f on E which assigns to $x \in E$ the s-measure of the arc connecting a to x. So $f(a) = 0$ and f increases as you move x along E away from a. Using the Whitney extension theorem,[2] f can be extended to all of $\mathbf{R}^2$. It turns out that the degree of differentiability of f is the same as the dimension of E. Hence f is continuously differentiable or C^1. Moreover, its gradient ∇f satisfies $\nabla f(x) = 0$ for any $x \in E$. This last assertion is easy for us to see: $|\nabla f(x)|$ is estimated by comparing the s-measure of small arcs of E containing x with their diameters. But we have already seen that the s-measure of an arc is comparable to its diameter raised to the power s. Since $s > 1$ if follows immediately that $\nabla f(x) = 0$.

This produces a C^1 function $f \colon \mathbf{R}^2 \to \mathbf{R}$ which is nonconstant on a connected set of critical points. You might ask, doesn't this contradict the fundamental theorem of calculus for gradients which should imply that

$$\int_E \nabla f \, ds = f(a) - f(b)$$

where $a \neq b$ are points of E? The problem is that our E is not smooth.

This example led Morse (1939) to prove a theorem which developed into the 'Morse-Sard' theorem.[3] Let us consider a special case:

THEOREM. *Let $f \colon \mathbf{R}^n \to \mathbf{R}$ be a C^r function and E a connected subset of R^n on which f is critical (i.e. $\nabla f = 0$ for all $x \in E$). If $r \geq n$ then f restricted to E is constant.*

Hence, the preceding example cannot be C^2.

Norton noticed that the differentiability class of f in the examples is exactly the dimension of the self-similar set. This led to his thesis result (1987) in which he showed that you can ignore the dimension of the domain of f in the generalized Morse-Sard theorem. All you need to know is that the Hausdorff dimension of the critical set E is not too big. Again, we consider only a special case for this exposition.

THEOREM.[4] *Let $f \colon \mathbf{R}^n \to \mathbf{R}$ be a C^r function and E a connected subset of R^n on which f is critical. If $r > \dim(E)$ then f restricted to E is constant.*

---

[2]The Whitney extension theorem is a 'converse' to Taylor's theorem. It provides necessary and sufficient conditions for a function and its 'candidate' derivatives defined on a closed set to have a smooth extension. It is naturally suited for fractal constructions (see Abraham and Robbin (1967) or Norton (1987).)

[3]**Theorem** (*see Sard* (1942)). *If $f \colon \mathbf{R}^n \to \mathbf{R}^m$ is C^k, A is a critical set for f and $k \geq \max\{1, m - n + 1\}$ then the m-dimensional Lebesgue measure of $f(A)$ is 0.*

Looking at the contrapositive, this theorem says that if you have a 'Whitney counterexample', the critical set must have dimension $\geq r$. So as r increases, the dimension of this fractal must also increase. It follows that

if $n - 1 < r < n$ then the critical set must be a fractal.

This is the opposite phenomenon that we saw for graphs in 4.1 where the dimension of the graph decreased with the differentiability of the function.

Here is an important clue to a way we might use fractals to prove theorems. In 5.1 we will see other examples where *the dimension of an assumed pathology is forced to be so large under a sufficiently smooth mapping that it cannot be contained in the space.*

4.3. Fractals are flexible. Let us consider a Whitney counterexample f of the previous section, defined on a neighborhood of an arc $E \subset \mathbf{R}^2$ such as the snowflake. Define $F(x,y) = (x + f(x,y), y)$. This mapping looks simple, but it has a strange property. Its total derivative DF is the identity matrix at all points of E. If E were smooth, we could conclude from the fundamental theorem of calculus that F has to translate E. That is, there exists $c \in \mathbf{R}^2$ such that $F(x) = c + x$ for all $x \in E$. However, you can easily see that there is no such c since f is not constant on E. What does the set $F(E)$ look like? Since DF is the identity, there can be no contraction or expansion or rotation locally. F is locally rigid.

If F is any mapping of the form

$$F(x,y) = (x + af(x,y), y + bf(x,y))$$

where $a, b \in \mathbf{R}$, we call the set $F(E)$ a *flexed image* of E. Note that the collection of all flexed images of an arc E forms a 2-parameter family depending only on E.

Some computer realizations of flexed images of fractals are shown in Figures 10 and 11 on page 122.

---

[4]Norton also showed that if $r \in \mathbf{Z}$ then $r \geq \dim(E)$ implies that f is constant on E. Thus, his theorem generalizes the Morse-Sard theorem. In fact, all of these results generalize considerably. (See Norton (1986).) It should be noted that the work is dual to results of Federer (1969) and Yomdin (1983) in which the dimension of the image of an arbitrary critical set is controlled independently of m. Norton suggested the following generalization to all of these results: If A has rank r for $f \in C^s$ and is t-null, $t \geq r$, then $f(A)$ is $(r + (t - r)/s)$-null.

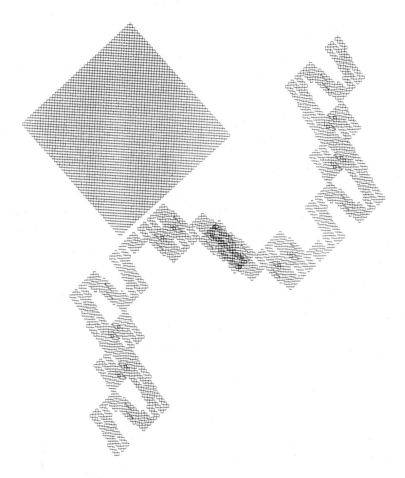

FIGURE 10. A detail of an approximation of the Peano curve and its flexed image under the mapping $F(x, y) = (x + f, y - f)$.

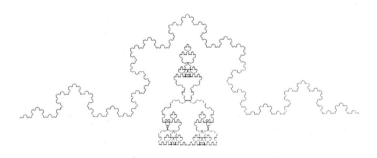

FIGURE 11. The snowflake and its flexed image under the mapping $F(x, y) = (x - f(x, y), y)$.

5. Fractals in dynamical systems.

5.1. Denjoy counterexamples. Suppose f is a diffeomorphism of a smooth manifold M. We say that a nonempty, compact set $E \subset M$ is *invariant* for f if $f(E) = E$. If E contains no other invariant sets then we call E *minimal*. Minimal sets are important because they form a 'skeleton' of the dynamics.

If M is the circle, then we completely understand what minimal sets can look like. Poincaré realized that there were only three possibilities for minimal sets for homeomorphisms of the circle S^1: they are either finite, the whole circle or a Cantor set. If the minimal set is a Cantor set, we call f a *Denjoy counterexample*. Although there exist C^1 Denjoy counterexamples, Denjoy (1932) proved there are no such C^2 examples.

Fractals can give us some insight into this. The simplest Denjoy counterexamples f that can be constructed have the property that the dimension of the minimal Cantor set increases with the degree of differentiability of f. Indeed, if the derivative $f' \in C^\varepsilon$, $0 < \varepsilon < 1$, then the dimension of the minimal Cantor set is at least ε (Harrison (1988c)). So as the degree of differentiability of f increases to two, the dimension of the minimal set increases to one.

Next we will see that this phenomenon has an analogue for diffeomorphisms on the two-sphere S^2 and vector fields on the three-sphere S^3.

THE LOXODROMIC MAPPING CONJECTURE. *Let $f: S^2 \to S^2$ be a diffeomorphism of S^2. Suppose f has only two periodic points—the north pole N which attracts and the south pole S which repels. If one orbit is asymptotic to both N and S then all orbits are asymptotic to N and S.*

It would follow that f is topologically conjugate (i.e., equivalent) to the standard loxodromic, or 'hot fudge', mapping. This conjecture is related to the celebrated question of Seifert (1950):

THE SEIFERT CONJECTURE. *Every vector field on S^3 has either zeros or closed integral curves.*

Schweitzer (1974) found C^1 counterexamples to this by using Denjoy counterexamples in a clever way. His method can be extended and generalized to the following.

THEOREM.[5] *If the Seifert Conjecture is true for vector fields of class C^r then the Loxodromic Mapping Conjecture is true for diffeomorphisms of class C^r.*

Here's where fractals come in. If you want to find a counterexample to the Loxodromic Conjecture—and hence a counterexample to the Seifert

---

[5]Harrison (1988c).

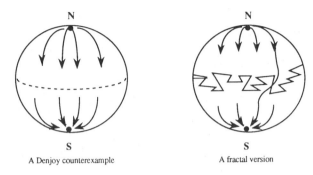

A Denjoy counterexample   A fractal version

FIGURE 12. Two counterexamples to the Loxodromic
Mapping Conjecture.

Conjecture—you have to create an infinite minimal set which is bounded
away from N and S and through which you can push points. You can use
the Denjoy counterexample as in Figure 12. Now that you are aware of the
link between dimension and differentiability it should come as no surprise
that by increasing the dimension of the circle you can also increase the differentiability of the mapping. (See Harrison (1988a)). The phenomenon that
begins on the circle continues on the sphere, but it stops at C^3. Moreover,
there is growing evidence that *any* counterexample to the Loxodromic Conjecture will face this obstruction. Thus Hausdorff dimension could provide
an important component to proving the Seifert Conjecture is *true* for C^3
vector fields.

5.2. Miscellaneous results. There have been volumes of results relating Hausdorff measure and dimension to dynamical systems. Our limited space won't
allow us to discuss these in any depth. We can just provide a few references.
Besides discoveries in the world of rational maps, we see in the work of Beardon (1966), Bowen (1979) and Sullivan (1983) that group actions often have
fractals in their structure. They can be attractors as in Grassberger (1981).
They arise as basin boundaries of attractors (Grebogi, Ott & Yorke (1987)).
They are built into the Smale horseshoe as in the work of McCluskey &
Manning (1983) and are related to entropy and Lyapunov exponents (Frederickson, Kaplan, Yorke & Yorke (1983) and Ledrappier & Young (1985)).
The boundary of the region where Newton's method is well defined can be a
fractal. (See Curry, Garnett, Sullivan (1983), for example.) One-dimensional
maps have fractals in them. (For a survey see Whitley (1983)). These are
just a few of the many areas of current research.

Much of the work on fractals in dynamical systems has yet to be put on
a rigorous foundation. Science beckons both new and seasoned mathematicians to validate, de-mystify and transform the experiments.

References

Barcellos, A., *The fractal geometry of Mandelbrot*, College Math. J. **15** (1984), 98–119.

Beardon, A. F., *The Hausdorff dimension of singular sets of properly discontinuous groups*, Amer. J. Math. **88** (1966), 722–736.

Berry, M. V. and Lewis, Z. V., *On the Weierstrass–Mandlebrot fractal function*, Proc. Roy. Soc. London Ser. A **370** (1980), 459–484.

Besicovitch, A. S., *On the fundamental geometrical properties of linearly measurable plane sets of points*, Math. Ann. **98** (1928), 422–464.

Besicovitch, A. S. and Ursell, H. D., *Sets of fractional dimensions*, J. London Math. Soc. **12** (1937), 18–25.

Bowen, R., *Hausdorff dimension of quasi-circles*, Inst. Hautes Études Sci. Publ. Math. **50** (1979), 259–273.

Cannon, J. D., *Topological, combinatorial and geometric fractals*, Amer. Math. Monthly (to appear).

Carleson, L., *Selected problems on exceptional sets*, Van Nostrand, Princeton, N.J., 1967.

Curry, J., Garnett, L., and Sullivan, D., *On the iterations of rational functions: Computer experiments with Newton's method*, Comm. Math. Phys. **91** (1983), 267–277.

Denjoy, A., *Sur les courbes définies par les équations différentielles à la surface du tore*, J. Math. Pures Appl. **11** (1932), 333–375.

Falconer, K., *The geometry of fractal sets*, Cambridge University Press, 1985.

Federer, H., *Geometric measure theory*, Springer, New York, 1947.

Frederickson, P., Kaplan, J., Yorke, E., and Yorke, J., *The Lyapunov dimension of strange attractors*, J. Differential Equations **49** (1983), 185–207.

Frostman, O., *Potential d'équilibre et capacité des ensembles avec quelques applications à la théorie des fonctions*, Meddel. Lunds. Univ. Mat. Sem. **3** (1935), 1–118.

Grassberger, P., *On the Hausdorff dimension of fractal attractors*, J. Statist. Phys. **26** (1981), 173–179.

Grebogi, C., Ott, E., and Yorke, J., *Basin boundary metamorphoses: changes in accessible boundary orbits*, Phys. D. **24** (1987), 243–262.

Harrison, J., *Continued fractals and the Seifert Conjecture*, Bull. Amer. Math. Soc. (N.S.) **13** (1985), 147–153.

_____, *Denjoy fractals*, Topology (1988 a) (to appear).

_____, *Geometry of algebraic continued fractals*, Proceedings of the York Conference on Number Theory and Dynamical Systems–(1987), London Math Soc. (1988 b) (to appear).

_____, *Dimension and differentiability in Denjoy counterexamples*, (1988 c) in preparation.

Hurewicz, W. and Wallman, H., *Dimension theory*, Princeton University Press, 1941.

Hutchinson, J. E., *Fractals and self similarity*, Indiana Univ. Math. J. **30** (1981), 713–747.

Kauffman, R., *On Hausdorff dimension of projections*, Mathematika **15** (1968), 153–155.

Kolmogorov, A. N., *ε-entropy and ε-capacity of sets in functional spaces*, Transl. Amer. Math. Soc. **17** (1961), 277–364.

Ledrappier, F. and Young, L. S., *The metric entropy of diffeomorphisms*, Ann. of Math. **122** (1985), 540–574.

Mandelbrot, B. B., *Les objets fractals: forme, hasard et dimension*, Flammarion, Paris, 1975.

_____, *Fractals: Form, chance, and dimension*, W. H. Freeman, San Francisco, 1977.

_____, *The fractal geometry of nature*, W. H. Freeman, New York, 1983.

Marstrand, J. M., *Some fundamental geometrical properties of plane sets of fractional dimensions*, Proc. London Math. Soc. (3) **4** (1954), 257–302.

Mattila, P., *On the structure of self-similar fractals*, Ann. Acad. Sci. Fenn. Ser. A **7** (1982), 189–195.

McCluskey, H. and Manning, A., *Hausdorff dimension for horseshoes*, Ergodic Theory Dynamical Systems **3** (1983), 251–260.

Morgan, F., *Geometric measure theory—A beginner's guide*, Academic Press, 1988.

Morse, A. P., *The behavior of a function on its critical set*, Ann. of Math. (2) **40** (1939), 62–70.

Norton, A., *A critical set with nonnull image has large Hausdorff dimension*, Trans. Amer. Math. Soc. **296** (1986), 367–376.

_____, *The fractal geometry of critical sets with nonnull image and the differentiability of functions*, thesis, Berkeley, 1987.

Ostrowski, N. and Stanley, H. E. editors, *On growth and form: Fractal and non-fractal patterns in physics*, M. Nijhoff, The Hague, 1985.

Peitgen, H.-O. and Richter, P. H., *The beauty of fractals, images of complex dynamical systems*, Springer, 1986.

Rogers, C. A., *Hausdorff measure*, Cambridge University Press, 1970.

Ruelle, D., *Repellers for real analytic maps*, Ergodic Theory Dynamical Systems **2** (1982), 99–108.

_____, *Bowen's formula for the Hausdorff dimension of self-similar sets*, Progr. Phys. **7** (1983).

Sard, A., *The measure of the critical values of differentiable maps*, Bull. Amer. Math. Soc. **48** (1942), 883–890.

Schweitzer, P., *Counterexamples to the Seifert conjecture and opening closed leaves of foliations*, Ann. of Math., (2) **100** (1974), 386–400.

Seifert, H., *Closed integral curves in 3-space and isotopic 2-dimensional deformations*, Proc. Amer. Math. Soc. **1** (1950), 287–302.

Stein, E., *Singular integrals and differentiability properties of functions*, Princeton University Press, 1970.

Stewart, I., *The chronicles of primrose polymath: Into the two and a halfth dimension*, Librairie Classique Eugene Belin, Paris, 1988, (preprint).

Sullivan, D., *Conformal dynamical systems*, Lecture Notes in Math., vol. 1007, Springer, 1983, pp. 725–752.

_____, *Quasiconformal homeomorphisms and dynamics* I–III, Inst. Hautes Études Sci. (preprint).

Tricot, C., *Douze définitions de la densité logarithmique*, C. R. Acad. Sci. Paris Sér. I Math. **293** (1981), 549–552.

_____, *Two definitions of fractional dimension*, Math. Proc. Cambridge Philos. Soc. **91** (1982), 57–74.

Whitley, D., *Discrete dynamical systems in dimensions one and two*, Bull. London Math. Soc. **15** (1983), 177–217.

Whitney, H., *A function non-constant on a connected set of critical points*, Duke Math. J. **1** (1935), 514–517.

Yomdin, Y., *The geometry of critical and near-critical values of differentiable mappings*, Math. Ann. **264** (1983), 495–515.

DEPARTMENT OF MATHEMATICS, UNIVERSITY OF CALIFORNIA, BERKELEY, CALIFORNIA 94720

Proceedings of Symposia in Applied Mathematics
Volume 39, 1989

Lecture Notes on Iterated Function Systems

MICHAEL F. BARNSLEY

ABSTRACT. This lecture provides an introduction to the theory and application of iterated function systems. Iterated function systems provide a convenient framework for the theory and communication of deterministic "fractals." The theory has two main components: (i) *geometric point-set topology*, which is concerned with the existence and characterization of certain invariant compact sets as fixed points of certain "simply described" contraction mappings on certain metric spaces whose points are compact sets; (ii) *measure theory*, which is concerned with the existence and description of certain normalized Borel measures as the fixed points of certain contraction mappings on some metric spaces whose elements are normalized Borel measures. The applications are in two main areas: (i) modelling of structures and data in the physical sciences; (ii) computer science, specifically to image compression, computer graphics, and communications.

INTRODUCTION

Geometry is concerned with making our spatial intuitions objective. Classical geometry provides a first approximation to the structure of physical objects; it is the language which we use to communicate the designs of technological products, and, very approximately, the forms of natural creations. Fractal geometry is an extension of classical geometry. It can be used to make precise models of physical structures from ferns to galaxies. Fractal geometry is a new language. Once you can speak it, you can describe the shape of a cloud as precisely as an architect can describe a house.

We begin by describing a metric space, denoted $\mathscr{H}$, whose elements are the nonempty compact subsets of a space such as $\mathbf{R}^2$. Under the right conditions $\mathscr{H}$ is complete, sequences converge, and fractals can be found!

Fractals are discovered as the fixed points of certain set maps. They are generated by the application of "simple" transformations on "simple" spaces. It is explained what an iterated function system (IFS) is, and how it can define a fractal. Iterated function systems provide a convenient framework for the description, classification, and communication of fractals. The inverse problem is considered: given a compact subset of $\mathbf{R}^2$ how does one go about

1980 *Mathematics Subject Classification* (1985 *Revision*). Primary 58F13.

finding a fractal approximation to it? Part of the answer is provided by the Collage Theorem. The thought of the wind blowing through a fractal tree leads to discovery of conditions under which fractals depend continuously on the parameters which define them.

We also consider measures on fractals. The space $\mathscr{P}$ of normalized Borel measures on a compact metric space is defined. With an appropriate metric, $\mathscr{P}$ becomes a compact metric space. Succinctly defined contraction mappings on this space lead to measures which live on fractals. Integrals with respect to these measures can be evaluated with the aid of Elton's ergodic theorem. The notes end with a brief description of the application of these measures to computer graphics.

We are concerned exclusively with *deterministic* geometry, which is useful for describing *specific* objects and structures. Models are represented by succinct "formulas." Once the formula is known the model can be reproduced. We do not consider statistical geometry. In deterministic geometry structures are defined, communicated, and analysed, with the aid of elementary transformations such as affine transformations, scalings, rotations, and congruences.

A fractal set generally contains infinitely many points whose organization is so complicated that it is not possible to describe the set by specifying directly where each point in it lies. Instead, the set may be defined by "the relations between the pieces." It is rather like describing the solar system by quoting the law of gravitation and stating the initial conditions. Everything follows from that. It appears always to be better to describe in terms of relationships.

A key reference to the material which follows is [**Hutc81**].

TOPOLOGY WITH GEOMETRY

The metric space $(\mathscr{H}(\mathbf{X}), h)$: The space where fractals live. We describe a good space in which to study fractal geometry. To start with, and always at the deepest level, we work in some complete metric space such as $(\mathbf{R}^2, \text{Euclidean})$ or $(\hat{\mathbf{C}}, \text{spherical})$, which we denote by $(\mathbf{X}, d)$. But then, when we wish to discuss pictures, drawings, "black-on-white" subsets of the space it becomes natural to introduce the space $\mathscr{H}$. Some elements of $\mathscr{H}(\mathbf{R}^2, \text{Euclidean})$ are suggested in Figure 1.

DEFINITION 1. Let $(\mathbf{X}, d)$ be a complete metric space. Then $\mathscr{H}(\mathbf{X})$ denotes the space whose points are the compact subsets of $\mathbf{X}$, other than the empty set.

DEFINITION 2. Let $(\mathbf{X}, d)$ be a complete metric space, $x \in \mathbf{X}$, and $B \in \mathscr{H}(\mathbf{X})$. Define

$$d(x, B) = \text{Min}\{d(x, y) : y \in B\}.$$

$d(x, B)$ is called the *distance from* the point x *to* the set B.

FIGURE 1

DEFINITION 3. Let $(\mathbf{X}, d)$ be a complete metric space. Let $A, B \in \mathscr{H}(\mathbf{X})$. Define

$$d(A, B) = \text{Max}\{d(x, B): x \in A\}.$$

$d(A, B)$ is called the *distance from* the set $A \in \mathscr{H}(\mathbf{X})$ *to* the set $B \in \mathscr{H}(\mathbf{X})$. Compare d(Georgia, U.S.A.) to d(U.S.A., Georgia). Let $(\mathbf{X}, d)$ be a complete metric space. Show that if A, B, and $C \in \mathscr{H}(\mathbf{X})$ then

$$d(A \cup B, C) = d(A, C) \vee d(B, C).$$

We use the notation $x \vee y$ to mean the maximum of the two real numbers x and y.

DEFINITION 4. Let $(\mathbf{X}, d)$ be a complete metric space. Then the *Hausdorff distance* between points A and B in $\mathscr{H}(\mathbf{X})$ is defined by

$$h(A, B) = d(A, B) \vee d(B, A).$$

Show that $h(A \cup B, C \cup D) \leq h(A, C) \vee h(B, D)$, for all A, B, C and $D \in \mathscr{H}(\mathbf{X})$.

LEMMA 1. *Let A and B be in $\mathcal{H}(\mathbf{X})$ where $(\mathbf{X}, d)$ is a metric space. Let $\varepsilon > 0$. Then*

$$h(A, B) \leq \varepsilon \Leftrightarrow A \subset B + \varepsilon \quad and \quad B \subset A + \varepsilon,$$

where $A + \varepsilon = \{x \in X : d(x, A) \leq \varepsilon\}$ is the "ε-dilation" of A.

Let $(\mathbf{X}, d)$ be a compact metric space. Show that $(\mathcal{H}(\mathbf{X}), h)$ is a compact metric space.

The completeness of the space of fractals. We refer to $(\mathcal{H}(\mathbf{X}), h)$ as "the space of fractals." It is too soon to be formal about the exact meaning of a "fractal." At the present stage of development of science and mathematics, the idea of a fractal is most useful as a broad concept. Fractals are not defined by a short legalistic statement, but by the many pictures and contexts which refer to them. For us any subset of $(\mathcal{H}(\mathbf{X}), h)$ is a fractal. However more meaning is suggested than is formalized.

THEOREM 1. *Let $(\mathbf{X}, d)$ be a complete metric space. Then $(\mathcal{H}(\mathbf{X}), h)$ is a complete metric space. Moreover, if $\{A_n \in \mathcal{H}(\mathbf{X})\}_{n=1}^{\infty}$ is a Cauchy sequence then*

$$A = \operatorname*{Lim}_{n \to \infty} A_n \in \mathcal{H}(\mathbf{X})$$

can be characterized as follows:

  $A = \{x \in \mathbf{X} :$ there is a Cauchy sequence $\{x_n \in A_n\}$ that converges to $x\}$.

Contraction mappings on the space of fractals. Let $(\mathbf{X}, d)$ be a metric space and let $(\mathcal{H}(\mathbf{X}), h(d))$ denote the corresponding space of nonempty compact subsets, with the Hausdorff metric $h(d)$. We introduce the notation $h(d)$ to show that d is the underlying metric for the Hausdorff metric h. For example, we may discuss $(\mathcal{H}(\hat{\mathbf{C}}), h(\text{spherical}))$ or $(\mathcal{H}(\mathbf{R}^2), h(\text{Manhattan}))$. We will drop this additional notation when we evaluate Hausdorff distances.

    The following lemma tells us how to make a contraction mapping on $(\mathcal{H}(\mathbf{X}), h(d))$ out of a contraction mapping on $(\mathbf{X}, d)$.

LEMMA 2. *Let $w: \mathbf{X} \to \mathbf{X}$ be a contraction mapping on the metric space $(\mathbf{X}, d)$ with a contractivity factor s. Then $w: \mathcal{H}(\mathbf{X}) \to \mathcal{H}(\mathbf{X})$ defined by*

$$w(B) = \{w(x): x \in B\} \quad \forall B \in \mathcal{H}(\mathbf{X})$$

is a contraction mapping on $(\mathcal{H}(\mathbf{X}), h(d))$ with contractivity factor s.

LEMMA 3. *For all $B, C, D,$ and E in $\mathcal{H}(\mathbf{X})$*

$$h(B \cup C, D \cup E) \leq h(B, D) \vee h(C, E)$$

where h is the Hausdorff metric.

    The next lemma provides an important method for combining contraction mappings on $(\mathcal{H}(\mathbf{X}), h)$ to produce new contraction mappings on $(\mathcal{H}(\mathbf{X}), h)$. This method is distinct from the obvious one of composition.

LEMMA 4. *Let* $(\mathbf{X}, d)$ *be a metric space. Let* $\{w_n : n = 1, 2, \ldots, N\}$ *be contraction mappings on* $(\mathscr{H}(\mathbf{X}), h)$. *Let the contractivity factor for* w_n *be denoted by* s_n *for each n. Define* $W : \mathscr{H}(\mathbf{X}) \to \mathscr{H}(\mathbf{X})$ *by*

$$W(B) = w_1(B) \cup w_2(B) \cup \cdots \cup w_N(B)$$

$$= \bigcup_{n=1}^{N} w_n(B), \quad \text{for each } B \in \mathscr{H}(\mathbf{X}).$$

Then W *is a contraction mapping with contractivity factor* $s = \text{Max}\{s_n : n = 1, 2, \ldots, N\}$.

DEFINITION 5. A (hyperbolic) *iterated function system* consists of a complete metric space $(\mathbf{X}, d)$ together with a finite set of contraction mappings $w_n : \mathbf{X} \to \mathbf{X}$, with respective contractivity factors s_n, for $n = 1, 2, \ldots, N$. The abbreviation "IFS" is used for "iterated function system". The notation for the IFS just announced is $\{\mathbf{X}; w_n, n = 1, 2, \ldots, N\}$ and its contractivity factor is $s = \text{Max}\{s_n : n = 1, 2, \ldots, N\}$. The nomenclature "iterated function system" is meant to remind one of the name "dynamical system."

THEOREM 2. *Let* $\{\mathbf{X}; w_n, n = 1, 2, \ldots, N\}$ *be a hyperbolic iterated function system with contractivity factor s. Then the transformation* $W : \mathscr{H}(\mathbf{X}) \to \mathscr{H}(\mathbf{X})$ *defined by*

$$W(B) = \bigcup_{n=1}^{N} w_n(B)$$

for all $B \in \mathscr{H}(\mathbf{X})$, *is a contraction mapping on the complete metric space* $(\mathscr{H}(\mathbf{X}), h(d))$ *with contractivity factor s. Its unique fixed point,* $A \in \mathscr{H}(\mathbf{X})$, *obeys*

$$A = W(A) = \bigcup_{n=1}^{N} w_n(A),$$

and is given by $A = \text{Lim}_{n \to \infty} W^{\circ n}(B)$ *for any* $B \in \mathscr{H}(\mathbf{X})$.

DEFINITION 6. The fixed point $A \in \mathscr{H}(\mathbf{X})$ described in the theorem is called the *attractor* of the IFS.

Here we have resisted the temptation to use the words "deterministic fractal" in place of "attractor."

The deterministic algorithm for computing fractals from iterated function systems. We ignore important questions concerning discretization and accuracy.

For simplicity we restrict attention to hyperbolic IFS of the form $\{\mathbf{R}^2; w_n : n = 1, 2, \ldots, N\}$, where each mapping is an affine transformation. We illustrate the algorithms for an IFS whose attractor is a Sierpinski triangle. The following is an example of such an IFS.

$$w_1 \begin{bmatrix} x_1 \\ x_2 \end{bmatrix} = \begin{bmatrix} 0.5 & 0 \\ 0. & 0.5 \end{bmatrix} \begin{bmatrix} x_1 \\ x_2 \end{bmatrix} + \begin{bmatrix} 1 \\ 1 \end{bmatrix},$$

$$w_2 \begin{bmatrix} x_1 \\ x_2 \end{bmatrix} = \begin{bmatrix} 0.5 & 0 \\ 0. & 0.5 \end{bmatrix} \begin{bmatrix} x_1 \\ x_2 \end{bmatrix} + \begin{bmatrix} 1 \\ 50 \end{bmatrix},$$

$$w_3 \begin{bmatrix} x_1 \\ x_2 \end{bmatrix} = \begin{bmatrix} 0.5 & 0 \\ 0 & 0.5 \end{bmatrix} \begin{bmatrix} x_1 \\ x_2 \end{bmatrix} + \begin{bmatrix} 25 \\ 50 \end{bmatrix}.$$

This notation for an IFS of affine maps is cumbersome. Let us agree to write

$$w_i(x) = w_3 \begin{bmatrix} x_1 \\ x_2 \end{bmatrix} = \begin{bmatrix} a_i & b_i \\ c_i & d_i \end{bmatrix} \begin{bmatrix} x_1 \\ x_2 \end{bmatrix} + \begin{bmatrix} e_i \\ f_i \end{bmatrix} = A_i x + t_i.$$

Then Table 1 is a tidier way of conveying the same iterated function system.

TABLE 1. IFS code for a Sierpinski triangle.

w	a	b	c	d	e	f	p
1	0.5	0	0	0.5	1	1	0.33
2	0.5	0	0	0.5	1	50	0.33
3	0.5	0	0	0.5	25	50	0.34

Table 1 also provides a number p_i associated with w_i for $i = 1, 2, 3$. These numbers are in fact probabilities. In the more general case of the IFS $\{X; w_n : n = 1, 2, \ldots, N\}$ there would be N such numbers $\{p_i : i = 1, 2, \ldots, N\}$ which obey

$$p_1 + p_2 + p_3 + \cdots + p_N = 1 \quad \text{and} \quad p_i > 0 \quad \text{for } i = 1, 2, \ldots, N.$$

These probabilities play an important role in the computation of images of the attractor of an IFS using the Random Iteration Algorithm. They play no role in the Deterministic Algorithm. Their mathematical significance is discussed in connection with measures on attractors of IFS.

Let $\{X; w_1, w_2, \ldots, w_N\}$ be a hyperbolic IFS. Choose a compact set $A_0 \subset \mathbf{R}^2$. Then compute successively $A_n = W^{0n}(A)$ according to

$$A_{n+1} = \bigcup_{j=1}^{N} w_j(A_n) \quad \text{for } n = 1, 2, \ldots.$$

Thus construct a sequence $\{A_n : n = 0, 1, 2, 3, \ldots\} \subset \mathscr{H}(X)$. Then by Theorem 2 the sequence $\{A_n\}$ converges to the attractor of the IFS in the Hausdorff metric.

We illustrate the implementation of the algorithm. The following program computes the plot's successive sets A_{n+1} starting from an initial set A_0, in this case a square, using the IFS code in Table 1. The program is written in BASIC. It should run without modification on an IBM PC with Color

Graphics Adaptor or Enhanced Graphics Adaptor, and Turbobasic. It can be modified to run on any personal computer with graphics display capability. On any line the words which are preceded by a ' are comments, they are not part of the program.

PROGRAM 1 (EXAMPLE OF THE DETERMINISTIC ALGORITHM).
screen 1. cls 'initialize graphics
dim $s(100, 100)$: dim $t(100, 100)$ 'allocate two arrays of pixels
$a(1) = 0.5$: $b(1) = 0$: $c(1) = 0$: $d(1) = 0.5$: $e(1) = 1$: $f(1) = 1$ 'input the
IFS code
$a(2) = 0.5$: $b(2) = 0$: $c(2) = 0$: $d(2) = 0.5$: $e(2) = 50$: $f(2) = 1$
$a(3) = 0.5$: $b(3) = 0$: $c(3) = 0$: $d(3) = 0.5$: $e(3) = 25$: $f(3) = 50$
for $i = 1$ to 100 'input the initial set $A(0)$, in this case a square, into the
array $t(i, j)$
$t(i, 1) = 1$: pset$(i, 1)$ '$A(0)$ can be used as a condensation set
$t(1, i) = 1$: pset$(1, i)$ '$A(0)$ is plotted in the screen
$t(100, i) = 1$: pset$(100, i)$
$t(i, 100) = 1$: pset$(i, 100)$
next: do
for $i = 1$ to 100 'apply W to set $A(n)$ to make $A(n + 1)$ in the array $s(i, j)$
for $j = 1$ to 100: if $t(i, j) = 1$ then
$s(a(1) * i + b(1) * j + e(1), c(1) * i + d(1) * j + f(1)) = 1$ 'and apply W to
$A(n)$
$s(a(2) * i + b(2) * j + e(2), c(2) * i + d(2) * j + f(2)) = 1$
$s(a(3) * i + b(3) * j + e(3), c(3) * i + d(3) * j + f(3)) = 1$
end if: next j: next i
cls 'clears the screen—omit to obtain sequence with a $A(0)$ as condensation
set (see Definitions 7 and 8 and Theorem 3 below)
for $i = 1$ to 100: for $j = 1$ to 100
$t(i, j) = s(i, j)$ 'put $A(n + 1)$ into the array $t(i, j)$
$s(i, j) = 0$ 'reset the array $s(i, j)$ to zero
if $t(i, j) = 1$ then
pset(i, j) 'plot $A(n + 1)$
end if: next: next
loop until instat 'if a key has been pressed then stop, otherwise compute
$A(n + 1) = W(A(n + 1))$

The result of running a variant of this program and then printing the contents of the graphics screen is presented in Figure 2. In this case we have kept nine successive images produced by the program.

Condensation sets. There is another important way of making contraction mappings on $\mathscr{H}(\mathbf{X})$.

DEFINITION 7. Let $(\mathbf{X}, d)$ be a metric space and let $C \in \mathscr{H}(\mathbf{X})$. Define a transformation $w_0: \mathscr{H}(\mathbf{X}) \to \mathscr{H}(\mathbf{X})$ by $w_0(B) = C$ for all $B \in \mathscr{H}(\mathbf{X})$. Then

FIGURE 2

w_0 is called a *condensation transformation* and C is called the associated *condensation set.*

Observe that a condensation transformation $w_0\colon \mathscr{H}(\mathbf{X}) \to \mathscr{H}(\mathbf{X})$ is a contraction mapping on the metric space $(\mathscr{H}(\mathbf{X}), h(d))$, with contractivity factor equal to zero, and that is possesses a unique fixed point, namely the condensation set.

DEFINITION 8. Let $\{\mathbf{X}; w_1, w_2, \ldots, w_N\}$ be a hyperbolic IFS with contractivity factor $0 \leq s < 1$. Let $w_0\colon \mathscr{H}(\mathbf{X}) \to \mathscr{H}(\mathbf{X})$ be a condensation transformation. Then $\{\mathbf{X}; w_0, w_1, \ldots, w_N\}$ is called a *hyperbolic IFS with condensation*, with contractivity factor s.

THEOREM 3. *Let $\{\mathbf{X}; w_n\colon n = 0, 1, 2, \ldots, N\}$ be a hyperbolic iterated function system with condensation, with contractivity factor s. Then the transformation $W\colon \mathscr{H}(\mathbf{X}) \to \mathscr{H}(\mathbf{X})$ defined by*

$$W(B) = \bigcup_{n=0}^{N} w_n(B) \quad \forall B \in \mathscr{H}(\mathbf{X})$$

COLOR PLATE 1

Color Plate 1 shows a colored Parameter Space for a one-parameter family of fern-like fractals, associated with an Iterated Function System. Inset are shown two of the corresponding Image Space ferns. Each point in the space corresponds to a different image, and can be thought of as a visual botanical classification scheme. This image was computed by Michael Barnsley and John Herndon, using the Escape Time Algorithm.
© Iterated Systems, Inc., Atlanta, GA, 1989.

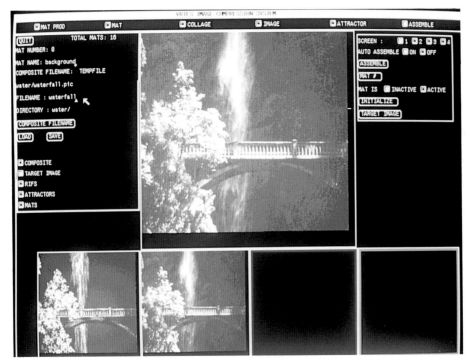

COLOR PLATE 2

Color Plate 2 shows a screen from the VRIFS[TM] *Image Compression System, together with images of a waterfall scene, before and after compression. Images are compressed by representing them using invariant measures of Iterated Functions Systems, as described in the article by Michael Barnsley. The attractor can be zoomed in upon for ever, revealing endless synthetic detail. VRIFS*[TM] *is a registered trade mark of Iterated Systems, Inc. © Iterated Systems, Inc., Atlanta, GA, 1989.*

is a contraction mapping on the complete metric space $(\mathscr{H}(\mathbf{X}), h(d))$ with contractivity factor s. That is

$$h(W(B), W(C)) \leq s \cdot h(B, C) \quad \forall B, C \in \mathscr{H}(\mathbf{X}).$$

Its unique fixed point $A \in \mathscr{H}(\mathbf{X})$ obeys

$$A = W(A) = \bigcup_{n=0}^{N} w_n(A)$$

and is given by $A = \mathrm{Lim}_{n \to \infty} W^{0n}(B)$ for any $B \in \mathscr{H}(\mathbf{X})$.

How to make fractal models with the help of the Collage Theorem. The following theorem is central to the design of IFSs whose attractors are close to given sets.

THEOREM 4 (THE COLLAGE THEOREM [**Barn85b**]). *Let* $(\mathbf{X}, d)$ *be a complete metric space. Let* $L \in \mathscr{H}(\mathbf{X})$ *be given, and let* $\varepsilon \geq 0$ *be given. Choose an IFS (or IFS with condensation)* $\{\mathbf{X}; (w_0), w_1, w_2, \ldots, w_N\}$ *with contractivity factor* $0 \leq s < 1$, *so that*

$$h\left(L, \bigcup_{\substack{n=1 \\ (n=0)}}^{N} w_n(L)\right) \leq \varepsilon,$$

where $h(d)$ *is the Hausdorff metric. Then*

$$h(L, A) \leq \varepsilon/(1 - s)$$

where A *is the attractor of the IFS. Equivalently,*

$$h(L, A) \leq (1 - s)^{-1} h\left(L, \bigcup_{\substack{n=1 \\ (n=0)}}^{N} w_n(L)\right) \quad \textit{for all } L \in \mathscr{H}(\mathbf{X}).$$

Figure 3 shows the attractor for an IFS $\{\mathbf{R}^3; w_i, i = 1, 2, 3, 4\}$ where each w_i is a three-dimensional affine transformation. The attractor is contained in the region $\{(x_1, x_2, x_3) \in \mathbf{R}^3 : -10 \leq x_1 \leq 10, 0 \leq x_2 \leq 10, -10 \leq x_3 \leq 10\}$.

FIGURE 3

$$w_1 \begin{bmatrix} x_1 \\ x_2 \\ x_3 \end{bmatrix} = \begin{bmatrix} 0 & 0 & 0 \\ 0 & 0.18 & 0 \\ 0 & 0 & 0 \end{bmatrix} \begin{bmatrix} x_1 \\ x_2 \\ x_3 \end{bmatrix} + \begin{bmatrix} 0 \\ 0 \\ 0 \end{bmatrix},$$

$$w_2 \begin{bmatrix} x_1 \\ x_2 \\ x_3 \end{bmatrix} = \begin{bmatrix} 0.85 & 0 & 0 \\ 0 & 0.85 & 0.1 \\ 0 & -0.1 & 0.85 \end{bmatrix} \begin{bmatrix} x_1, \\ x_2 \\ x_3 \end{bmatrix} + \begin{bmatrix} 0 \\ 1.6 \\ 0 \end{bmatrix},$$

$$w_3 \begin{bmatrix} x_1 \\ x_2 \\ x_3 \end{bmatrix} = \begin{bmatrix} 0.2 & 0.2 & 0 \\ 0.2 & 0.2 & 0 \\ 0 & 0 & 0.3 \end{bmatrix} \begin{bmatrix} x_1 \\ x_2 \\ x_3 \end{bmatrix} + \begin{bmatrix} 0 \\ 0.8 \\ 0 \end{bmatrix},$$

$$w_4 \begin{bmatrix} x_1 \\ x_2 \\ x_3 \end{bmatrix} = \begin{bmatrix} -0.2 & 0.2 & 0 \\ 0.2 & 0.2 & 0 \\ 0 & 0 & 0.3 \end{bmatrix} \begin{bmatrix} x_1 \\ x_2 \\ x_3 \end{bmatrix} + \begin{bmatrix} 0 \\ 0.8 \\ 0 \end{bmatrix}.$$

Blowing in the wind: The continuous dependence of fractals on parameters. The Collage Theorem provides a way of approaching the inverse problem: Given a set L, find an IFS for which L is the attractor. The underlying mathematical principle is very easy: the proof of the Collage Theorem is just the proof of the following lemma.

LEMMA 5. *Let* $(\mathbf{X}, d)$ *be a complete metric space. Let* $f: \mathbf{X} \to \mathbf{X}$ *be a contraction mapping with contractivity factor* $0 \leq s < 1$, *and let the fixed point of* f

be $x_f \in \mathbf{X}$. Then

$$d(x, x_f) \le (1 - s)^{-1} \cdot d(x, f(x)) \quad \text{for all } x \in \mathbf{X}.$$

Theorem 5. *Let $(\mathbf{X}, d)$ be a metric space. Let $\{\mathbf{X}; (w_0), w_1, w_2, \ldots, w_N\}$ be a hyperbolic IFS (with condensation), of contractivity s. For $n = 1, 2, \ldots, N$, let w_n depend continuously on a parameter $p \in P$, where P is a compact metric space. Then the attractor $A(p) \in \mathscr{H}(\mathbf{X})$ depends continuously on $p \in P$, with respect to the Hausdorff metric $h(d)$.*

In other words, small changes in the parameters will lead to small changes in the attractor, provided that the system remains hyperbolic. This is very important because it tells us that we can continuously control the attractor of an IFS, by adjusting parameters in the transformations, as is done in image compression applications. It also means we can smoothly interpolate between attractors: this is useful for image animation, for example.

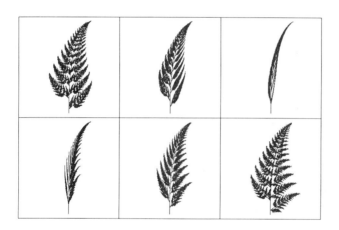

FIGURE 4

MEASURE THEORY

Measures on fractals which can be represented by iterated function systems. We focus on measures which arise from iterated function systems in $\mathbf{R}^2$.

Below we introduce the Random Iteration Algorithm. This algorithm is a means for computing the attractor of a hyperbolic IFS in $\mathbf{R}^2$. In order to run the algorithm one needs a set of probabilities, in addition to the IFS.

Definition 9. An iterated function system *with probabilities* consists of an IFS $\{\mathbf{X}; w_1, w_2, \ldots, w_N\}$ together with an ordered set of numbers $\{p_1, p_2, \ldots, p_N\}$, such that

$$p_1 + p_2 + p_3 + \cdots + p_N = 1 \quad \text{and} \quad p_i > 0 \quad \text{for } i = 1, 2, \ldots, N.$$

The probability p_i is associated with the transformation w_i. The nomenclature "IFS with probabilities" is used for "iterated function system with probabilities." The full notation for such an IFS is $\{\mathbf{X}; w_1, w_2, \ldots, w_N; p_1, p_2, \ldots, p_N\}$. Explicit reference to the probabilities may be suppressed.

We introduce an exciting metric space. It is the space where fractals *really* live.

DEFINITION 10. Let $(\mathbf{X}, d)$ be a compact metric space. Let μ be a Borel measure on $\mathbf{X}$. If $\mu(\mathbf{X}) = 1$ then μ is said to be *normalized.*

DEFINITION 11. Let $(\mathbf{X}, d)$ be a compact metric space. Let $\mathscr{P}(\mathbf{X})$ denote the set of *normalized Borel measures* on $\mathbf{X}$. The *Hutchinson metric* d_H on $\mathscr{P}(\mathbf{X})$ is defined by

$$d_H(\mu, \nu) = \text{Sup}\left\{\int_{\mathbf{X}} f d\mu - \int_{\mathbf{X}} f d\nu : \right.$$

$$f: \mathbf{X} \to \mathbf{R} \text{ is continuous, and obeys}$$

$$\left. |f(x) - f(y)| \le d(x, y) \, \forall x, y \in \mathbf{X}\right\},$$

for all $\mu, \nu \in \mathscr{P}(\mathbf{X})$.

THEOREM 6. *Let $(\mathbf{X}, d)$ be a compact metric space. Let $\mathscr{P}(\mathbf{X})$ denote the set of normalized Borel measures on $\mathbf{X}$ and let d_H denote the Hutchinson metric. Then $(\mathscr{P}(\mathbf{X}), d_H)$ is a compact metric space.*

A contraction mapping on $\mathscr{P}(\mathbf{X})$. Let $(\mathbf{X}, d)$ denote a compact metric space. Let $\mathscr{B}$ denote the Borel subsets of $\mathbf{X}$. Let $w: \mathbf{X} \to \mathbf{X}$ be continuous. Then one can prove that $w^{-1}: \mathscr{B} \to \mathscr{B}$. It follows that if ν is a normalized Borel measure on $\mathbf{X}$ then so is $\nu \circ w^{-1}$. In turn, this implies that the function defined next indeed takes $\mathscr{P}(\mathbf{X})$ into itself.

DEFINITION 12. Let $(\mathbf{X}, d)$ be a compact metric space and let $\mathscr{P}(\mathbf{X})$ denote the space of normalized Borel measures on $\mathbf{X}$. Let $\{\mathbf{X}; w_1, w_2, \ldots, w_N; p_1, p_2, \ldots, p_N\}$ be a hyperbolic IFS with probabilities. The *Markov operator* associated with the IFS is the function $M: \mathscr{P}(\mathbf{X}) \to \mathscr{P}(\mathbf{X})$ defined by

$$M(\nu) = p_1 \nu \circ w_1^{-1} + p_2 \nu \circ w_2^{-1} + \cdots + p_N \nu \circ w_N^{-1}$$

for all $\nu \in \mathscr{P}(\mathbf{X})$.

LEMMA 6. *Let M denote the Markov operator associated with a hyperbolic IFS, as in Definition 12. Let $f: \mathbf{X} \to \mathbf{R}$ be either a simple function or a continuous function. Let $\nu \in \mathscr{P}(\mathbf{X})$. Then*

$$\int_{\mathbf{X}} f d(M(\nu)) = \sum_{i=1}^{N} p_i \int_{\mathbf{X}} f \circ w_i \, d\nu.$$

THEOREM 7. *Let $(\mathbf{X}, d)$ be a compact metric space. Let $\{\mathbf{X}; w_1, w_2, \ldots, w_N; p_1, p_2, \ldots, p_N\}$ be a hyperbolic IFS with probabilities. Let $s \in (0, 1)$ be a contractivity factor for the IFS. Let $M: \mathscr{P}(\mathbf{X}) \to \mathscr{P}(\mathbf{X})$ be the associated Markov* *operator. Then M is a contraction mapping, with contractivity factor s, with respect to the Hutchinson metric on $\mathscr{P}(\mathbf{X})$. That is,*

$$d_H(M(\nu), M(\mu)) \leq s d_H(\nu, \mu) \quad \text{for all } \nu, \mu \in \mathscr{P}(\mathbf{X}).$$

In particular, there is a unique measure $\mu \in \mathscr{P}(\mathbf{X})$ such that

$$M\mu = \mu.$$

DEFINITION 13. Let μ denote the fixed point of the Markov operator, promised by Theorem 1. μ is called the *invariant measure* of the IFS with probabilities.

We have arrived at our goal! *Now* we know what fractals are.

THEOREM 8. *Let $(\mathbf{X}, d)$ be a compact metric space. Let $\{\mathbf{X}; w_1, w_2, \ldots, w_N; p_1, p_2, \ldots, p_N\}$ be a hyperbolic IFS with probabilities. Let μ be the associated invariant measure. Then the support of μ is the attractor of the IFS $\{\mathbf{X}; w_1, w_2, \ldots, w_N\}$.*

THEOREM 9 (THE COLLAGE THEOREM FOR MEASURES). *Let $\{\mathbf{X}; w_1, w_2, \ldots, w_N; p_1, p_2, \ldots, p_N\}$ be a hyperbolic IFS with probabilities. Let μ be the associated invariant measure. Let $s \in (0, 1)$ be a contractivity factor for the IFS. Let $M: \mathscr{P}(\mathbf{X}) \to \mathscr{P}(\mathbf{X})$ be the associated Markov operator. Let $\nu \in \mathscr{P}(\mathbf{X})$. Then*

$$d_H(\nu, \mu) \leq \frac{d_H(\nu, M(\nu))}{(1 - s)}.$$

We conclude with a description of the application of Theorem 8 to an inverse problem. The problem is to find an IFS with probabilities whose invariant measure, when represented by a set of dots, looks like a given texture.

A measure supported on a subset of $\mathbf{R}^2$ such as ⊡ can be represented by a lot of black dots on a piece of white paper. The dots may be granules of carbon attached to the paper by means of a laser printer. The number of dots inside any circle of radius $\frac{1}{2}$ inch, say, should be approximately proportional to the measure of the corresponding ball in $\mathbf{R}^2$. A greytone image in a newspaper is made of small dots and can be thought of as representing a measure.

Let two such images, each consisting of the same number of points, be given. Then we expect that the degree to which they look alike corresponds to the Hutchinson distance between the corresponding measures.

Let such an image, L, be given. We imagine that it corresponds to a measure ν. Theorem 9 can be used to help to find a hyperbolic IFS with probabilities whose invariant measure, represented with dots, approximates the given image. Let N be a positive integer. Let $w_i: \mathbf{R}^2 \to \mathbf{R}^2$ be an affine transformation, for $i = 1, 2, \ldots, N$. Let $\{\mathbf{R}^2; w_1, w_2, \ldots, w_N; p_1, p_2, \ldots, p_N\}$ denote the sought-after IFS. Let M denote the associated Markov operator.

Let $p_i \& L$ mean the set of dots L after the "density of dots" has been decreased by a factor p_i. For example $0.5 \& L$ means L after "every second dot" in L has been removed. The action of the Markov operator on ν is represented by $\bigcup_{i=1}^{N} w_i(p_i \& L)$. This set consists of approximately the same number of dots as L. Then we seek contractive affine transformations and probabilities such that

(†)
$$\bigcup_{i=1}^{N} w_i(p_i \& L) \approx L.$$

That is, the coefficients which define the affine transformations and the probabilities must be adjusted so that the left-hand side "looks like" the original image.

Suppose we have found an IFS with probabilities so that (†) is true. Then generate an image $\tilde{L}$ of the invariant measure of the IFS, containing the same number of points as L. We expect that

(‡)
$$\tilde{L} \approx L.$$

If the maps are sufficiently contractive, then the meaning of "$\approx$" should be the same in both (†) and (‡).

Elton's ergodic theorem. The theorem below is actually true when the p_is are functions of x, the w_is are only contraction mappings "on the average" and the space is locally compact.

THEOREM 10. *Let $(\mathbf{X}, d)$ be a compact metric space. Let $\{\mathbf{X}; w_1, w_2, \ldots, w_N; p_1, p_2, \ldots, p_N\}$ be a hyperbolic IFS with probabilities. Let $(\mathbf{X}, d)$ be a compact metric space. Let $\{x_n\}_{n=0}^{\infty}$ denote an orbit of the IFS produced by the Random Iterative Algorithm, starting at x_0. That is,*

$$x_n = w_{\sigma_n} \circ w_{\sigma_{n-1}} \circ \cdots \circ w_{\sigma_1}(x_0),$$

where the maps are chosen independently according to the probabilities $p_1, p_2, \ldots, p_N$, for $n = 1, 2, 3, \ldots$. Let μ be the unique invariant measure for the IFS. Then with probability one (that is, for all code sequences $\sigma_1, \sigma_2, \ldots$ except for a set of sequences having probability zero),

$$\lim_{n \to \infty} \frac{1}{n+1} \sum_{k=0}^{n} f(x_k) = \int_{\mathbf{X}} f(x) \, d\mu(x)$$

for all continuous functions $f \colon \mathbf{X} \to \mathbf{R}$ and all x_0.

PROOF. See [Elto86].

COROLLARY 1. *Let B be a Borel subset of $\mathbf{X}$ and let $\mu(boundary \ of \ B) = 0$. Let*

$$\mathcal{N}(B, n) = number \ of \ points \ in \ \{x_0, x_1, x_2, x_3, \ldots, x_n\} \cap B,$$

for $n = 0, 1, 2, \ldots$. Then, with probability one,

$$\mu(B) = \lim_{n \to \infty} \left\{ \frac{\mathcal{N}(B, n)}{(n+1)} \right\}$$

for all starting points x_0. That is, the "mass" of B is the proportion of iteration steps, when running the Random Iteration Algorithm, which produce points in B.

The Random Iteration Algorithm. Let $\{X; w_1, w_2, \ldots, w_N\}$ be a hyperbolic IFS, where probability $p_i > 0$ has been assigned to w_i for $i = 1, 2, \ldots, N$, where $\sum_{i=1}^{N} p_i = 1$. Choose $x_0 \in X$ and then choose recursively, independently,

$$x_n \in \{w_1(x_{n-1}), w_2(x_{n-1}), \ldots, w_N(x_{n-1})\} \quad \text{for } n = 1, 2, 3, \ldots,$$

where the probability of the event $x_n = w_i(x_{n-1})$ is p_i. Thus construct a sequence $\{x_n : n = 0, 1, 2, 3, \ldots\} \subset X$.

The sequence $\{x_n\}_{n=0}^{\infty}$ "converges to" the attractor of the IFS, under various conditions, in a manner which can be made precise with the aid of Elton's ergodic theorem.

We illustrate the implementation of the algorithm. Program 2 below computes and plots a thousand points on the attractor of the IFS code at the start of the program. The program is written in BASIC. It runs without modification on an IBM PC with Enhanced Graphics Adaptor and Turbobasic.

PROGRAM 2 (EXAMPLE OF THE RANDOM ITERATION ALGORITHM).

```
a[1] = 0.5: b[1] = 0: c[1] = 0: d[1] = .5: e[1] = 1: f[1] = 1   'Iterated
Function System Data
a[2] = 0.5: b[2] = 0: c[2] = 0: d[2] = .5: e[2] = 50: f[2] = 1
a[3] = 0.5: b[3] = 0: c[3] = 0: d[3] = .5: e[3] = 25: f[3] = 50
screen 1: cls   'initialize computer graphics
window (0, 0) - (100, 100)   'set plotting window to 0 < x < 1, 0 < y < 1
x = 0: y = 0: numits = 1000   'initialize (x, y) and define the number of
iterations, numits
for n = 1 to numits   'Random Iteration begins!
k = int(3 * rnd - 0.00001) + 1   'choose one of the numbers 1, 2, and 3 with
equal probability
'apply affine transformation number k to (x, y)
newx = a[k] * x + b[k] * y + e[k]: newy = c[k] * x + d[k] * y + f[k]
x = newx: y = newy   'set (x, y) to the point thus obtained
if n > 10 then pset (x, y)   'plot (x, y) after the first 10 iterations
next: end
```

Output from the program, after slight changes in the data, is shown in Figure 5.

APPLICATIONS

Application to computer graphics. We begin by explaining how a color image of the invariant measure of an IFS with probabilities, can be produced. The idea is very simple. We start from an IFS such as

$$\{C; 0.5z + 24 + 24i, 0.5z + 24i, 0.5z; 0.25, 0.25, 0.5\}.$$

A viewing window and a corresponding array of pixels P_{ij} is specified. The Random Iteration Algorithm is applied to the IFS, to produce an orbit $\{z_n : n = 0, 1, \ldots, numits\}$, where $numits$ is the number of iterations. For each (i, j)

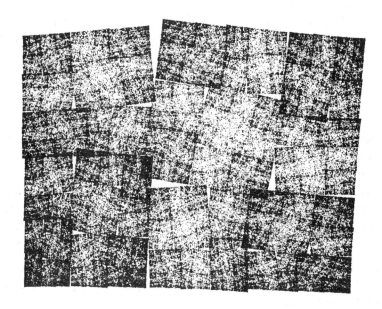

FIGURE 5

the number of points, $\mathcal{N}(P_{ij})$, which lie in the pixel P_{ij}, are counted. The pixel P_{ij} is assigned the value $\mathcal{N}(P_{ij})/numits$. By Elton's theorem, if *numits* is large, this value should be a good approximation to the measure of the pixel. The pixels are plotted on the screen in colors which are determined from their measures.

"Pictures" of invariant measures of IFSs possess a number of properties. (i) Once the viewing window and color assignments have been fixed, the image produced is stable with respect to the number of iterations, provided that the number of iterations is sufficiently large. (ii) Images vary consistently with respect to translation and rotation of the viewing window, and with respect to changes in resolution. In particular they vary consistently when they are magnified. (iii) The images depend continuously on the IFS code, including the probabilities. Properties (i) and (ii) are consequences of corresponding properties Borel of measures on $\mathbf{R}^2$. Property (iii) follows from a theorem by Withers [**With87**].

Property (i) ensures that the images are well defined. The properties in (ii) are also true for views of the real world seen through the viewfinder of a camera. Property (iii) means that images can be controlled interactively. These properties suggest that IFS theory is applicable to computer graphics.

Applications of fractal geometry to computer graphics have been investigated by a number of authors. The focus has been on the modelling of natural objects and scenes. Both deterministic and random geometries have been used. The application of IFS theory to computer graphics was first reviewed in [**Demk85**]. It provides a single framework which can reach an unlimited range of images. It is distinguished from other fractal approaches because it is the only one which uses measure theory.

The modelling of natural scenes is an important area of computer graphics. Photographs of natural scenes contain redundant information in the form of subtle patterns and variations. There are two characteristic features. They are (i) the presence of complex geometrical structure and distributions of color and brightness at many scales; and (ii) the hierarchical layout of objects. (i) Natural boundaries and textures are not smoothed out under magnification; they preserve some degree of geometrical complexity. (ii) Natural scenes are organized in hierarchical structures. For example a forest is made of trees; a tree is a collection of boughs and limbs along a trunk; on each branch there are clusters of leaves; and a single leaf is filled with veins and covered with fine hairs. It appears often in natural scenes that a recognizable entity is built up from numerous near repetitions of some smaller structure. These two observations can be integrated into systems for modelling images using IFS theory.

In [**Barn88a**] it is reported that IFS theory can be used efficiently to model photographs of clouds, mountains, ferns, a field of sunflowers, a forest, seascapes and landscapes, a hat, the face of a girl, and a glaring arctic wolf.

Applications to image compression and communications. IFS codes can provide a succinct means for representing images. Automatic systems which the output IFS codes for digitized images are being developed for commercial use. Compressed images can be transmitted rapidly. Special purpose devices can regenerate images at high speeds.

REFERENCES

[**Barn85a**] M. F. Barnsley and S. Demko, *Iterated function systems and the global construction of fractals*, Proc. Roy. Soc. London Ser. A **399** (1985), 243–275.

[**Barn85b**] M. F. Barnsley, V. Ervin, D. Hardin, and J. Lancaster, *Solution of an inverse problem for fractals and other sets*, Proc. Nat. Acad. Sci. U.S.A. **83** (1985).

[**Barn86a**] M. F. Barnsley, *Fractal functions and interpolation*, Constructive Approximation **2** (1986), 303–329.

[**Barn88a**] M. F. Barnsley, A. Jacquin, L. Reuter, and A. D. Sloan, *Harnessing chaos for image synthesis*, Computer Graphics (SIGGRAPH 1988 Conference Proceedings).

[**Barn88b**] M. F. Barnsley and A. D. Sloan, *A better way to compress images*, Byte Magazine, January 1988, pp. 215–223.

[**Barn88c**] M. F. Barnsley, *Fractals everywhere*, Academic Press/Harcourt Brace Jovanovitch, 1988.

[**Barn88d**] M. F. Barnsley and J. Elton, *A new class of Markov processes for image encoding*, J. Appl. Probab. **20** (1988), 14–32.

[**Bedf86**] T. J. Bedford, *Dimension and dynamics for fractal recurrent sets*, J. London Math. Soc. (2) **33** (1986), 89–100.

[**Brol66**] H. Brolin, *Invariant sets under iteration of rational functions*, Ark. Mat. **6** (1966), 103–144.

[**Demk85**] S. Demko, L. Hodges, and B. Naylor, *Construction of fractal objects with iterated function systems*, Computer Graphics (3) **19** (1985), 271–278.

[**Dekk82**] F. M. Dekking, *Recurrent sets*, Adv. in Math. **44** (1982), 78–104.

[**Diac86**] P. M. Diaconis and M. Shahshahani, *Products of random matrices and computer image generation*, Contemp. Math. **50** (1986), 173–182.

[**Elto86**] J. Elton, *An ergodic theorem for iterated maps*, Ergodic Theory Dynamical Systems **7** (1987), 481–488.

[**Gilb82**] W. J. Gilbert, *Fractal geometry derived from complex bases*, Math. Intelligencer **4** (1982), 78–86.

[**Hard86**] D. P. Hardin and P. Massopust, *Dynamical systems arising from iterated function systems*, Comm. Math. Phys. **105** (1986), 455–460.

[**Hata85**] M. Hata, *On the structure of self-similar sets*, Japan J. Appl. Math. **2** (1985), 381–414.

[**Hutc81**] J. Hutchinson, *Fractals and self-similarity*, Indiana Univ. J. Math. **30** (1981), 713–747.

[**Mand82**] B. Mandelbrot, *The fractal geometry of nature*, Freeman, San Francisco, 1982.

[**Peit86**] H.-O. Peitgen and P. H. Richter, *The beauty of fractals*, Springer-Verlag, Berlin and New York, 1986.

[**Reut87**] L. Reuter, *Rendering and magnification of fractals using iterated function systems*, Ph.D. Thesis, Georgia Institute of Technology, December 1987.

[**Sina76**] Ya. G. Sinai, *Introduction to ergodic theory*, Princeton University Press, 1976.

[**Sull82**] D. Sullivan, *Quasi conformal homeomorphisms and dynamics*, I, II, and III, Inst. Hautes Etudes Sci., Bures-sur-Yvette, France, 1982 (preprints).

[**With87**] W. D. Withers, *Calculating derivatives with respect to parameters of average values in iterated function systems*, Phys. D **28** (1987), 206–214.

SCHOOL OF MATHEMATICS, GEORGIA INSTITUTE OF TECHNOLOGY, ATLANTA, GEORGIA 30332

ITERATED SYSTEMS INC., 5550-A PEACHTREE PARKWAY, NORCROSS, GEORGIA 30092

Index